PRAISE FOR MAR

The Ruby Heart of the Dragon

Deep thinking about astrological theory side by side with the examined life are an unbeatable combo platter. In *The Ruby Heart of the Dragon*, Mark Borax deftly weaves astrological autobiography into a fresh, and very evolutionary, perspective on the twelve signs. A big plus is that he has the craft of a true writer—there's music in his language too.

STEVEN FORREST, AUTHOR OF *THE INNER SKY*

I've been a professional astrologer for 50 years. I thought I knew just about all there was to know about the zodiac, but *The Ruby Heart* offers an entirely new perspective. Mark Borax's descriptions of the signs, put forth with crystal clarity, are mind-bending. I devoured this book, which I recommend to anyone: novice or well-seasoned, because there is so much new knowledge to take from it.

STEPHANIE AZARIA, CREATOR OF *THECOSMICPATH.COM* AND *COSMIC CONSCIOUSNESS*

If you are looking for a book on Sun signs that captures the differences between people born in each of the signs, consider *The Ruby Heart of the Dragon: Sun Signs for Our Times*. This is not an abstract work on the mechanics of the astrological signs, it is a telling in little stories of the author's zodiac observations that is both insightful and poetic.

BRUCE SCOFIELD, AUTHOR OF *DAY SIGNS* AND OTHER BOOKS ON MESOAMERICAN ASTROLOGY

This is a book to return to again and again.

DEBORAH KOFF-CHAPIN, CREATOR OF *SOUL CARDS 2*

2012: Crossing the Bridge to the Future

Mark Borax has given us a vision of the future that is as hopeful as it is radical. He is proposing nothing less than that we are beginning to heal the cosmic breach from which all of our other problems—ecological, political, social, spiritual—originate.

RICHARD GROSSINGER, AUTHOR OF *THE BARDO OF WAKING LIFE*

Cosmic Weather Report: Guidance for Radically Changing Times (with Ellias Lonsdale)

I highly recommend Mark Borax to all pioneers working toward the conscious evolution of ourselves and our world.

BARBARA MARX HUBBARD, AUTHOR OF *CONSCIOUS EVOLUTION: AWAKENING OUR SOCIAL POTENTIAL*

*For information about the audiobook and
ebook editions of this work, please visit*

therubyheartofthedragon.com

THE
RUBY HEART
OF
THE DRAGON

THE
RUBY HEART
OF THE
DRAGON

SUN SIGNS
FOR
OUR TIMES

MARK BORAX

DINANDA BOOKS  PUTNEY, VERMONT

Published by Dinanda Books
P.O. Box 623
Putney, Vermont 05346

Cover art and design by Peter Selgin
Page design by Chinook Design, Inc.

Printed in the United States of America

ISBN 979-8-9877711-0-5 (print)
ISBN 979-8-9877711-1-2 (ebook)

Library of Congress Cataloging-in-Publication Data

Borax, Mark, 1954

The Ruby Heart of the Dragon : sun signs for our time / Mark Borax

ISBN 979-8-9877711-0-5

1. Astrology. 2. Spirituality 3. Self-help 4. Philosophy

therubyheartofthedragon.com

CONTENTS

This book presumes no former knowledge of astrology but is about much more than its text. To read between the lines, open your third eye—but don't close the other two!

What can we gain by sailing to the moon if we are not able to cross the abyss that separates us from ourselves?

Thomas Merton

Introduction:
Awakening the Dragon

ANCIENT PEOPLE SAW THE WORLD AS A RAVAGING MONSTER that can only be tamed by the soul force within you, which remains dormant like a sleeping dragon till you cross the abyss between you and yourself. Astrology, though it often stumbles into lazy thinking, when practiced as a high visionary art is one of the best methods I know of for awakening the dragon.

The zodiac is a creation story that proposes twelve variations on the theme of being human, twelve quests for individuation, twelve life arts, twelve invitations to awaken. It's a tale spun in antiquity, revised many steps along the way. At every stop the zodiac picked something up and dropped something off, becoming a melting pot of world history and culture.

Unlike most tales, the zodiac is a story without an ending, because it's still being written. To update the narrative for these challenging times I've remodeled the signs by dismantling their clichés, stripping them down to core, and building them back up again.

When someone asks what your astrology sign is, they're referring to the sign the Sun appeared to be passing through when you were born. Along with your Sun sign you have two other crucial signs—the one you're leaving behind and the one you're heading toward. Arabian astrologers lent provocative names to the north and south nodes of the Moon, the karmic points where the Moon's orbit crosses the path of the Sun. They called your south node, which contains issues left over from your past and from your past lives, the dragon's tail, and the opposite point of the north node they called the dragon's head, which indicates the true north of your life, the destiny your soul came back to create.

Birth charts contain many other features, but this volume is concerned with the deep karma-yoga stretch from the dragon's tail to its head, that leads through its heart. Based on your birthday, you can identify those nodal signs using the tables in the back of this book. When you turn to those tables, be aware that you're not looking up your Sun sign but two other signs very important to you.

I see your astrological Sun as a ruby heart, which stimulates the warm emanation of your innermost being and empowers you to shine your creative purpose into the world. Like the sun in the sky, your inner Sun radiates growth rays that impel you to become the whole of who you are. Depending on which sign the Sun was passing through at the time of your birth, those rays shine upon the world from one of a dozen angles.

HOW TO USE THIS BOOK

Your Dragontail, Sun sign and Dragonhead represent your past, present and future. The more you resolve unfinished business at the tail end, the more your ruby heart flashes a laser beam into the territory ahead. The more progress you make going forward, the less binding is the heavy tail of the past.

Awakening the dragon also awakens your life art, because every life is an art, no less complex and transformative than painting, sculpture or music. We're all works in progress with underlying themes, recurring mysteries and splendid breakthroughs. We all have our own way of seeing things, which we don't usually consider an art because nobody told us to. We often take our most unique qualities for granted, unless someone sees into us clearly enough to point them out, which is one of the main reasons I wrote this book.

In art, unlike algebra, there are no right or wrong answers. But there are remedial and masterful methods of practicing your life art, preliminary graspings and profound discoveries, which the following pages divide by the number twelve. Each chapter is designed as a travelogue through the mysterious and provocative territory of a single sign, a mythic country with its own borders, perils and revelations. To bring the stars down to Earth I dip into my personal adventures through those lands, in some chapters more than others.

Chapters conclude with a paragraph that outlines what it means to have that sign as the head or tail of your dragon. The old country you're departing from and the promised land up ahead are equally worth contemplating, because so far as I can tell, the road to enlightenment runs three steps forward and two steps back. Until you gain a strong sense of what you're moving out of, it's hard to know what you're moving into.

Even if a particular sign isn't part of your dragon, you can learn more about the sign by reading how it manifests as the head and tail of someone else's dragon, which makes the final chapter pages the spice that enhances the main dish of information served up in the chapter. A third variation of the signs can be found in the afterword, which draws the twelve together in a way designed to launch your flight.

Because each sign builds upon previous signs and sets up subsequent ones, I suggest reading the entire book in chronological order, to grasp how your stage of the journey fits with the rest, then going back and rereading about your three main signs. Since everyone contains the whole zodiac in some unique mash-up, you'll probably find pieces of yourself scattered like dragon scales throughout the pages.

Reading the book aloud to someone you care about (perhaps yourself) is recommended, because while reading chapters in progress to friends born in those signs, I found the fuller scope of the material responding to vocalization (which enabled me to practice for recording the audio version). To get the most from my words you should consider them not the final say on the zodiac, but signposts to point you toward your own insights and revelations.

Unlike much astrology information my aim here is not to tell you what to do. You won't find much of that kind of advice. The Soul Level Astrology I practice differs from other kinds by assuming that a core part of you knows who you are and what you need more than I ever could. Instead of telling you what to do my aim is to activate the part of you that already knows. If my writing makes it that far into you and stimulates your inner knowing, I'll feel content that I've done my job. This type of starwork requires more of your collaboration and takes more time to mature in you than other kinds. As with thought-provoking literature or poetry you may wish to highlight sections of the text and return to them later.

Sexuality is one of the main themes I explore in my excavation of the twelve signs. You may have read a book about lovemaking or attended webinars or weekend workshops on sex. You may have gained intriguing concepts and provocative ideas. None of those, however, is the same as lovemaking. You could spend your life attending workshops and reading books—or you could make love. My exploration of the zodiac is similar because none of the tales and ideas I offer here will be complete within themselves until you embody your own unique blend of them.

As you press on into the exotic and familiar lands of the zodiac, you'll probably find yourself occasionally pausing, as if you'd been trudging through the jungle and suddenly came face to face with an ornate temple or breathtaking landscape. Like a transformative music experience or lovemaking session, the stories in the following pages, however compelling they may be, are not so important in themselves as they are in their potential to initiate your own magic. If you find new avenues of thought opening in the days and months ahead, this book will become the gift that goes on giving long after you close the cover.

Working on this manuscript for four years propelled me farther than I'd ever gone into the depths of the zodiac. Each day at my desk the signs never stopped morphing, and I never stopped huffing to catch up to them. Excavating like this launched me on a medicine journey I haven't come out of yet. I'm not sure I want to come out, so I guess you better come in, 'cause I could use the company.

Mark Borax
Putney Mountain, Vermont
Spring Equinox, 2023
The Year of the Cat

Note: Sun signs, unlike how they're described in newspapers, don't begin and end the same day each month, year after year, but can vary between the 19th and the 25th, so if you're in doubt, you should look up your birth day and year, and in some cases, your birth time, in a trustworthy source, or consult an astrologer. A few clients who've come to me for readings were shocked to learn they weren't the sign they thought they were.

CHAPTER ONE

The first sign doesn't precipitate out of thin air like Athena fully grown from the head of Zeus, but, like life on Earth did, emerges from the sea.

The zodiac (Arabic for "circle of animals") describes twelve variations of human nature that are also stages of consciousness we cycle through. The Piscean sea of merged consciousness completes the cycle and gives way in Aries to the light of a new dawn, which begins the journey all over again.

Out of spirit comes matter. Out of cosmos came Earth. Out of the collective fusion that occurs at the end of the zodiac comes the quest for individuation that starts it off, which will undergo many twists and turns before making it back to the sea.

Aries is on fire to prove it's alive, a thing of its own, separate from what came before: raw desire at its most basic, freshly arrived and stoked to learn what everything's about.

Aries isn't one of the more elaborate and sophisticated signs. Being first, it's not about making sure all is in place, but simply getting things off to a good start.

Along with initiating the twelve-stage journey, the forward thrust of Aries occasionally launches other momentums, some that reinforce its progress, and some that reinforce Newton's Third Law of Motion, which states that for every action there's an equal and opposite reaction. Like a young ram, Aries often learns what something's about by bashing into it and seeing what happens.

Finger Pointing
at the Moon:
The Zen Art of Aries

A S THE OPENING STATEMENT OF THE ZODIAC, ARIES launches a course of action the universe can't help responding to, often in unexpected ways, which Aries finds itself having to scramble through by the grace of good intentions and beginner's luck.

Raring to go, Aries is the early response unit of the zodiac, firing off snap decisions that occasionally land it in trouble, a destination many sheep become familiar with long before the age of consent.

When Aries tackles projects with clearly delineated parameters, few signs will go so far so fast. Lacking the defined initiative of such projects, Aries may sink into lethargy or mischief, which is why this sign seldom allows itself to run out of things to do—an idle ram is simply asking for trouble.

Aries thrives when motorized, and fumes when railroad barricades swing down and it's forced to wait, tapping its fingers on the steering wheel with smoke pouring out of its ears.

Shark of the zodiac, the sign often behaves as if its existence depends on keeping going (if sharks stop swimming, even while asleep, they die).

Named after the Greek god of war, Aries is prone to take umbrage when life bogs down in quagmires, as if they're personal insults that must be avenged by forward motion.

Astrologers sometimes associate Aries with the titan Prometheus (Forethought), who dared scale Mount Olympus to steal fire from the gods: the son challenging the father, the feminist challenging the patriarchy, the progressive urge of humanity overthrowing the old guard.

Though often strongly motivated, rams may only have a vague idea of what they're setting in motion, and even less idea of all they'll have to go through to get where they're going. But what this sign lacks in planning it more than makes up for with high energy and bright spirits. The unbridled exuberance of the first sign draws creative forces out of the ethers into the physical, where the ongoing question becomes what to do with them.

Each sign inherits a gift from the previous, which it transforms during its own stage of the journey, then passes to the next. From the final sign Pisces, the first sign inherits divine restlessness—the sea is always in motion. But unlike the pendulumatic motion of the tides, Aries blazes a trail forward and rarely looks back; most people born under the sign of the sheep are allergic to looking back.

Pisces is the mystic repository in the final stop of the zodiac, the alchemical alembic that sloshes the world body back and forth, while Aries is the burst of energy that jets out of the water like an otter bursting onto the shoreside path dashing uphill to its tribe.

Aries is the one in you who knows life's a discovery walk that comes alive the moment you do.

Aries is new life emerging in early spring, the crisp action that follows indecision, the 'I am' force compelling you to enter existence with avid participation.

If zodiac signs were parts of speech, the first would be a verb; Aries is not so much a thing as an action.

Even though number one is a self-directed sign, such inroads aren't cut for itself alone. After stealing Zeus's thunder, Prometheus didn't keep fire to himself but brought it down the mountain to the mortals who toiled in the shadow of the gods, to help humanity advance out of the dark ages (something we're still working on).

For his impudence, the rebellious titan was chained to a rock on command of Zeus, where an eagle (Zeus himself in one of his many shapes) ate Prometheus's liver each morning. Overnight it grew back, and the following day was eaten again, until eventually Hercules, during the eleventh of twelve labors, freed the long-suffering titan.[1]

So much sharp directed force is superlative for getting things moving. But constant pushing can make you toxic, which is what happens if your liver gets eaten. If Aries follows its battling namesake to the exclusion of other deities, its forward thrust is bound to backfire.

However, along with war, Aries was god of surgery; the same edge that makes a sword can make a scalpel, and many people born under this sign are prone to put their own needs aside to consider the needs of others.

When the premier sign learns that measuring how alive you are by how much controversy you create is a poor strategy for long-term success, it calls upon healing powers more than fight-or-flight instinct.

Its path to maturity leads toward recognizing how the physics of its ambition combine with the effects of personal actions upon a larger sphere of influence. It's fine for Aries to set sights on what it wants and go straight for it, as long as it realizes there are other things in the universe worth considering.

Struggling through trial-and-error growth pains that take more time to digest than this impatient sign usually wants to spend tends to produce one of two behavioral modifications that can alter its emotional capacity and worldview:

1. self-embattlement, where, feeling burned by the world, Aries pulls up the drawbridge that would let anyone in or out of its fortress; or
2. self-expansion, which grows experiential wisdom for Aries to see beyond the moat to the broader view and long-term arc of its growth.

---

[1] The labors of Hercules, along with the zodiac itself, are one of the many twelves that recur through history around the world: tribes of Israel, disciples of Jesus, days of Christmas, months of the year, to name a few. Cultures and religions as diverse as ancient Babylon, Judaism, Egypt, Rome, Islam, Hinduism, Buddhism and Zoroastrianism feature key examples of twelve, which is often considered (along with its multiple, 360) the number of the Whole. Astrology is largely based on these two numbers.

The latter can open the floodgates of all this exuberant sign has to offer, generating an inclusive energy that draws cohorts, supporters and allies.

Learning such lessons of self-enclosure and release can mature those born under the sign of Aries into first-rate mentors, whose restless spirits and learned patience equip them to speak to the restless and impatient spirits of others, especially those of the young.

As this young-at-heart sign learns more and more about the world around it, and about how its actions affect not just its own life but the rest of the universe, the fair-minded and noble aspects of the sign get carved out of its faux pas.

A ram who comes to understand not just the mechanics of doing but the science of its own nature (and everyone's nature is at least in one important way unique) sometimes becomes a golden fleece, contributing something worthwhile that raises the bar of aspiration for others.

Its devotion to a worthy cause can make Aries the most heroic sign. When its heroism outgrows the superficial idealism of youth and tunnel vision of zealots, the youngest sign begins to grow up.

Much Aries development comes from paying attention to its many experiences in the school of life, which is the main form of education likely to make sense to this hard-driving, sharp-edged opening act of the twelve-part play.

Lessons learned in the school of hard knocks regarding the subject matter of how to relate well with others while getting your own needs met go a long way toward polishing the sign's rough edges.

Later signs will make good use of the raw finds of Aries, but for now its rawness is exactly what the doctor ordered to get the zodiac off and running. When it learns from its bashes and blunders, the primal power of Aries can be directed toward incisive instant analyses of situations other signs might get tangled in.

Similar to how a person grows to their fullest when someone strongly believes in them, anything Aries focuses positive attention on is likely to flourish. Aries itself flourishes by strongly believing in itself without getting hung up on itself.

When the attention of this sign lags, it can get caught in the rising whine of an engine redlining in neutral. Somewhere inside that crescendo pistons are pumping, sparks are flying and exhaust is pouring out, but nothing's going anywhere.

Lack of enthusiasm or focus is a sure sign that some relationship, job or life context is no longer fueling this energetic sign. With such high idling, Aries either needs to get in gear and haul ass, or dig down to learn if some deeper engagement with a situation is possible.

The answer may be found by approaching choice points less like intellectual analysis stations and more like electrical wiring. This sign has so much bright urgency to connect that its restless energies seek outlets as avidly as electricity seeks a circuit. Once the circuit is rewired by Aries connecting to whatever it needs to connect with, and grounded by the grace of strong, clear intentions, the free flow of its energies almost always shows it the way to go.

Regardless of how stuck an Aries gets, how rattled or mystified, once this sign imagines itself more as a verb than a noun—less of a thing and more as energies stored up looking for a place to happen—it cuts complications by breaking down the equation of which way to go into something it can sizzle through instead of analyze and deliberate over.

Even though this restless sign doesn't always get where it starts out going, that's not likely to flounder it so much as give it a pinball bumper to rebound off and keep going. Though if it bounces around too much it's likely to get out of control and plunk down the gutter.

But it'll come back as soon as somebody pulls the plunger and fires the next ball up the alley and around the ramp for another go at life, another shot at love, another turn of the wheel.

Sometimes the goals of this goal-oriented sign turn out transitory or ephemeral. The constructive forces those searches set in motion, however, can have long-term shelf life, especially when they draw helpmates to aid this sign's solo searching.

In the 1980s when I started submitting comic book scripts to publishers, I found an ally in the only agent who represented comics writers and artists, Mike Friedrich, who happens to be an Aries.

True to his sign, Mike blew away the Old Guard of the industry by fighting for creators to get well-paid for their work, and start to gain a percentage of the lucrative licensing funds that were lining publishers' pockets, while chaining artists like Jack Kirby to their drawing boards, cranking out daily page rates for a pittance.

If a publisher was reluctant to relinquish control, Mike encouraged his clients to consider leaving that company and working for another, or joining the growing stable of independent writers and artists Mike assembled when he became the first publisher granting creators full rights, by launching Star * Reach comics.

Though I'm not an Aries, in my late twenties I was bursting with Aries-like energy to make a name for myself. Since my teens I'd had poems, articles and stories published, and had made a few bucks selling gags to Hallmark cards, but my lifelong dream to author a book kept starting to manifest and slipping away through the ethers almost as much as my love life did. So I reined some of that dream in and aimed it toward launching a comic book series.

I began tackling superhero plots, cobbling together treatments for J'onn J'onzz, Martian Manhunter; Hawkman and Hawkgirl; Batman, the Metal Men and many more, as well as my own creations, none of which sold. Eventually I wrote a one-shot science fiction script, *I Shot the Last Martian*, as an homage to Ray Bradbury, which Mike placed at Eclipse Comics for my first comics sale.

Mike told me that even though most of my tales wouldn't get sold, each submission opened the door to crafting relationships that could easily outlast any particular story I might be obsessing on.

He schooled me to recognize an unsold submission as the first stepping stone of a professional odyssey rather than something I should lose sleep over. I shouldn't think of selling scripts so much as buying relationships, and, above all, no matter how much rejection I got I needed to stay positive, especially when talking to editors.

Of course, as a young writer hot under the collar I didn't want to hear that my stories might not get sold! But his advice paid off when I stayed positive and Marvel bought a Fantastic Four time-traveling love story from me.

Intuiting the most direct path from *here* to *there,* Aries is the geometric line of the zodiac, reducing complications to the shortest distance between two points. Delays that trip up other signs evaporate in the friction lines of an Aries on top of its game, whose ability to cut to the quick can be rallying.

Because Aries is the first responder of the zodiac, it tends to generate momentum others like to get in on. When friends or allies appear, Aries can form partnerships that compensate for its personal blind spots, rounding out the narrowness of its linear thinking with the complexity of the surrounding view.

Sheep may seem distant, and not easy to read behind their mad dashes and knowing smiles, but if you gain the respect of an Aries, they're likely to cover your back and bristle at any injustices you suffer.

You can sometimes infer how much an Aries believes in you by how much space they grant you. The sign isn't likely to stand on ceremony, as an Aries values personal freedom over social niceties. Its greatest compliment may be to give you no compliment at all, to stand back and let you do your stuff.

Idealistic and romantic, driven by instinct, impatient with red tape, Aries is the part of us at odds with the delayed gratification and indirect results of *Technotopia Moderna.*

The forthrightness of this sign is the kind of approach that flourished in the straightforward culture of days gone by, when direct connections abounded and a camaraderie of the mind was fostered in classrooms, on porch rockers and around after-dinner tables.

In our day, simple, clear, direct encounters and conversations that encourage speakers to really listen and to open their minds to new ideas have become so rare they're almost extinct. Everybody gets so caught up in keeping everything going they have little left for good old-fashioned dialog.

Sometimes Aries becomes so focused on the task at hand it steamrolls over potential allies that could help it thrive or prevent it from making blunders. Recognizing the gifts of others enough to take cues from them is a frequent traffic redirection for the do-it-yourself sign of the zodiac.

However, some rams are difficult to reason with and impossible to slow down or redirect. That might not work out disastrously, depending on the accuracy of their aim, subtlety of their thought and their ability to read people.

Instinct runs strong in the early part of the zodiac, where sophisticated understandings and subtle thinking don't usually come naturally but are hard-won and dearly bought.

An Aries who augments its forward drive with subtle thinking may become skilled at correcting its course midstream, like paddling a canoe through surging whitewater.

But when instinct dominates an Aries who lacks subtle thought and surround vision, the intensity of their drive can make them overshoot their mark or capsize their canoe.

Though Aries gains a lot of mileage running on grit and friction, its maturity depends on easing up on conflict as a way to jump-start its battery, and finding smoother alternatives in order to get up the full head of steam it needs to go all the way into wherever it's going.

People-reading skills, though not usually this sign's natural-born talent, come in very handy because some people need no hand-holding and benefit from clear requests and instructions, whereas others need heavy maintenance if you wish to draw them along.

An Aries good at reading people can adjust how much force it applies compared to how much grace and diplomacy. People-reading skills help sheep preserve their mountain-moving power for when most needed.

A thriving Aries can be one of the most positive and productive members of the zodiac. Since Aries is almost always moving strongly in a certain direction, if you feel affinity with that direction and are interested in going along, in the blink of an eye Aries will be more than happy to sweep you in its wake.

The V-shaped formation of migrating geese conserves the flock's energy, because each bird flies slightly above the one in front, reducing wind drag, which allows every other bird to rest its wings while the others carry the load, until they trade off. Similarly, with Aries, when the movement of a certain group augments its own momentum, the premier sign can end up gliding along, directing the action or focusing the group.

Many Aries individuals have a strong relationship to words, and when they apply the same crisp economy of motion to their clarity of expression as they apply to achieving their goals, they can snap productivity and meaning in place as briskly as a set of Legos.

I have an Aries jeweler friend, Scott, who in the late 1990s was once dining in a booth next to the one I was sharing with Chris, another Aries friend of mine, at a Santa Cruz breakfast cafe. I'd been going through a sequence of crises (which I'll get into in a minute). I told Chris I felt like a boxer who, every time he barely gets up off the mat, gets whomped down again. I said I was reeling and blurted out that I wanted to get to the opposite of crisis, whatever that might be.

Recalling Scott had a way of clearing mental underbrush and cutting to the quick, I knocked on the little glass partition between our booths and said, "Hey Scott—what's the opposite of crisis?"

Instead of being put off by this out-of-the-blue question he took in my request with a slight nod, closed his eyes, went somewhere inside himself, then said, "Harvest."

Bingo! If I couldn't stop getting battered, I at least needed to find some way to draw the crises into harvest.

Although I'm Libra, the sign opposite Aries, Aries is at the root of my birth chart, the sign at the very bottom, foundational to my existence. You could say Aries is the ground I walk on. Libra tends to be as complex as Aries is simple. Libra weighs and balances, checks and measures, ponders and philosophizes, while Aries acts.

I needed to summon the full firepower of my Aries root at that time because I'd been laid low by a two-year onslaught in which my uncle died, my father died, my grandmother died, and my mother.[2]

---

[2] This chapter of my life began two years after the closing scene of my book *2012: Crossing the Bridge to the Future,* soon to be republished as *Love, Sex and Astrology.*

As if the deaths weren't enough, I also suffered a health setback and financial loss.

Two days after the harvest/crisis in the restaurant, Wendy, the woman I was deeply in love with and had been living with, told me she was going to move out.

I was dumbfounded.

Sitting on the hardwood floor, holding hands and facing each other, I fought to make sense of this continuing nightmare.

I don't get it, I said, because—wasn't she still in love with me like she always told me?

Yes, she replied.

Had I done something to diminish her feelings?

No.

Isn't our relationship as magic and awesome as we always say it is?

Yes.

Is our sex still beyond belief?

You know it is—you'll never find anyone to make love with the way we do.

Then—how can you go? Why would you leave?

After a long pause, when the very room seemed to be holding its breath, she shrugged. I don't know, Mark, she said—I guess your heart's just bigger than mine.

I tried to find a place inside myself that could fathom what this meant.... A bigger heart. *Does that mean a smaller brain?*

I wondered if it were true, this big heart, and how long it had taken her to figure out, and if there was anything I could do about it. I'd thought we were having a rough spot but not the end.

We'd been living in a cottage in the Santa Cruz Mountains, which we called the hobbit hole, perched directly over a little bend in the San Lorenzo River, where, with a sheepish look in her eyes, Wendy pried her fingers out of mine and stood to go.

After a long hug that I had trouble ending she walked to the door and gazed soulfully back at me while dramatic theme music poured through my head.

I flashed on a cinematic rescue, where, instead of standing there like a sawn Redwood about to topple, I'd run after her, tap her shoulder, and to the chorus of Van Morrison's "Crazy Love," she'd change her mind, rush into my arms and the credits would roll.

It didn't happen.

Robotically packing my things into cardboard boxes the next few dreary days and sleepless nights, I kept telling myself something right must be going on beneath so many things that seemed so wrong.

From being knocked down and climbing back up so much I'd come to believe the universe runs on some mystic interconnectedness I couldn't explain, but sensed had to be there.

Blow after blow after blow was anything but random. There had to be some message in the barrage, some meaning to the pattern. I knew loss after loss couldn't go on forever, but meanwhile, where was my life?

My life had always been volatile and unpredictable, now suddenly it had become even more volatile and all-too-predictable. If I could find the method to the madness, maybe I could start to harvest the crisis.

I thought about the Zen parable of the hermit who lives in a cave with only sandals, begging bowl and robe, and contemplated a similar course of action.

Returning from bathing in the river, the hermit finds a thief making off with the robe and sandals. He rushes after him holding up the bowl, shouting, "You forgot *this*!"

In similar fashion, at age forty-three when so much was being stripped away, I decided that instead of grasping to put things back, to go the opposite direction and release even more. So I gave away or sold my books, clothes, journals, musical instruments and CDs. With each trip to relinquish a load, I felt psychic weight lift, till I could walk past bookstores and music shops without feeling the slightest pull.

I went on the San Francisco radio show, atop a wharf-side skyscraper, that I'd used for ten years to build my astrology career, announced I was letting go of my practice, leaving the Bay Area and, like the Fool in a tarot deck, leaping into the unknown.

From my family's deaths I received a modest inheritance, which I took advantage of to keep a twenty-five-year promise to myself: that if I could ever afford it I'd buy a big Harley. I chose a brand-new, 1998 black-and-chrome Low Rider off the showroom floor (which I dubbed Blackie), hopped in the saddle and was off.

With no parents, grandparents, lover, home nor job; no cell phone nor schedule; no one to answer to and no possessions other than what I packed on Blackie (including my mother's ashes), like that Zen monk I went naked into the world, raw and reeling, with no conception of what should happen next.

I got rid of my watch because I had nothing but time. I was dazed and confused but free, or so I told myself several times a day, while waiting for the punch-drunk haze of Santa Craze to wear off and the magic of the road to kick in.

It was a strange bliss to not know where I'd sleep each night, where I'd end up and who I'd meet. Hanging onto my handlebars like the forked ends of a divining rod, all I had to do was keep one wheel in front of the other, as I dowsed the white-striped highway to some unknown destination.

If I wanted to turn left I'd turn left. If I wanted to go right I'd go right. If I wanted to keep going I could ride all night. If I fell in love with someone I could pull over and spend the rest of my life there.

There was nothing to answer to but the rhythm of the road and the thrumming gas tank I laid my chest on to feel direct connection with everything my tires touched, as I flew through a world that rose up and streamed behind me in monochrome and Technicolor.

At a Boston Harley shop I had Blackie crated to ship to London, then flew across the Atlantic. From England I rode through the tunnel to France, Belgium and Holland, then up and over the Alps into Italy, where I rented a quiet inexpensive apartment with marble floors in the medieval hilltop city of Bibiene, in Tuscany, between Florence and Siena.

In that bucolic and storied setting I settled down to catch my breath, gain my bearings and allow time to begin whatever healing it had in store.

I spent days walking the streets, cruising around on Blackie, writing songs and looking for my life, as if it were a lost cat I might find around the corner some afternoon along the grass strip where the old men played bocce ball, or in the alley beside the heavenly smells of fresh-baked bread.

Mornings I gazed from my small balcony to the distant silhouette of the mountain a nobleman had gifted Saint Francis for his woodland ministry. It wasn't Assisi, where his more famous church is, that I was looking at, but La Verna, off in the Apennines, site of his original chapel and still-functioning monastery.

Instead of an archetypal triangular mountain, La Verna's left side is a vertical rock wall that climbs to the structure's highest peak, then gradually slopes down like a long ramp stretching to the right, where it ends in a shorter vertical wall that parallels the one opposite. I took to sketching that ramp, which began calling through my dreams.

Since Mom always wanted to go to Europe, where her parents came from, but never made it, on the last day of September—her birthday—I rode Blackie up into the mountains.

In the dark, tiny, rough-hewn chapel with dirt floor, I knelt down and touched the mattress-sized and -shaped slab of solid rock, about a foot thick, that Francis slept on with no blanket or pillow. I felt stale energies whooshing out of me as if by vacuum cleaner, which made me feel this was the real deal. Sometimes at supposedly sacred sites I get nothing at all, but in that rustic chapel I was buzzing, and Francis's great and tender spirit seemed hard at work, flushing my system and eroding the numbness.

Back in the parking lot I unbuckled my saddlebag, took the sack of ashes and made my way through the forest. At the edge of the cliff I'd been gazing at from afar, I tipped the sack and poured the ashes out to where they sparkled in the breeze. Their flight over the mountain was my mother's last dance.

At the end of my Italian year I shipped Blackie to Los Angeles and continued my ride. One late morning in the Spring of 2000 I found myself in Sedona, Arizona, rooming at a friend's house, feeling rootless, displaced and hungry for female companionship.

I decided to take a day trip over Mingus Mountain to the historic wild-west town of Prescott, seeking a cigar and a woman, hoping the wind on my face or a possible romantic intrigue might lift my spirits.

I pulled on my boots, fired up Blackie and rode over the mountain to the edge of Prescott, where I spied a curvaceous woman with platinum hair, in a tight ice-blue dress, leaning against a street sign, as if luring me like a film noir siren.

Easing the throttle I gazed at her and she gazed back, then I told myself it was too good to be true, and accelerated to pass by.

Just before passing I braked, pulled over and asked if she wanted a ride. She hopped on, said her name was Gloria, wrapped her thighs around me, and asked if I wanted a beer at the corner bar. After beers she asked me to take her home.

We got on Blackie and she directed me through several turns toward the outskirts of town, down a long curving hill, up another, through more dips and turns, into a sprawling housing development, where she had me stop in front of a nondescript tract house that looked like the others.

We went in and she poured me orange juice, then filled a small pipe with ganja that she lit and we shared. She put Sade's "Smooth Operator" on the stereo, went into the bedroom, came out in a peach-colored nightgown, and we slow-danced in the kitchen.

After everything I'd gone through prior to my two-year ride, and everything I'd gone through since, that kitchen dance was surreal, as though I'd stumbled into a movie about some guy who happened to be me.

As we glided over the linoleum Gloria held me close, and said she made jewelry. She whispered she was in love with my necklace—a striking piece I'd picked out in Albuquerque during the early part of my ride. The necklace reminded me of Mom because of its showpiece of five fire opals, which, when I was a child, she'd told me was my birthstone.

Those azure gems, strung on a silver chain between black-enameled silver-barrel beads, were of rare depth and brilliance, with ruby flames in their core. Many people I'd met on my ride had seemed hypnotized, and it took me a long moment to realize they were staring at my necklace rather than me.

Impulsively I unclasped the chain and placed it around Gloria's neck, blue opals flashing against her platinum hair.

"What are you doing?! No, *I can't*—," she said as I fastened it.

She broke away, turned off the music and said, "Look. I gotta tell you. I brought you here under false pretexts."

"Huh?"

"The truth is, I'm gay. I know you're interested in me, but I gotta tell you it's not gonna go that way. Okay? Is that cool? You can stay if you want. I'll cook you an egg but then I gotta go to work."

I thought about it, shrugged, and said okay.

After the meal she told me it was time to go. At the front door she gave me her phone number, which I pocketed.

I got in the saddle, fired up Blackie, lost my bearings in the neighborhood, asked a kid for directions, then rode back to Sedona before placing my hand on my throat and realizing I'd forgotten the necklace. When I reached my friend's home I phoned Gloria and left a message for her to call so I could retrieve it.

After three days when she didn't call, I phoned again. She picked up and said she was meeting friends at a bowling alley that night where I could come get the piece. Adding that her plans were sketchy, she said she'd call back to confirm. She never did.

Four days went by with me leaving messages she didn't answer. The next morning I awoke with the realization she had no intention of returning the necklace.

I lay in bed fuming, till I realized anger was pouring out of me that I could channel into direct action, Aries-style, instead of taking the more Libran approach of batting the situation around in my head.

Though I didn't know if I could make good on it, I felt the trail to the necklace was imprinted in some Aries zone of consciousness in me, which knew the shortest distance between my current whereabouts and the jewels. Having no hypnotist at hand, I decided to navigate by Zen and outrage, like a finger pointing at the moon.

I fired up my bike and rode to Prescott, where I somehow managed to make my way to Gloria's neighborhood. I parked around the corner so she wouldn't hear the roar of my engine before I switched it off.

I walked to the house, pressed the buzzer, and waited. She opened the door wearing the gems, then flinched, recognizing me. I held out my hand palm-up and said, "Give me my necklace."

Trembling, she unclasped it and handed it over, muttering, "I was gonna give it back, ya know."

I walked away saying nothing. When I got to Sedona I saw she'd removed beads and shortened the chain to fit her neck.

Aries is the *ki* in Aikido, the *shakti* in Tantra, the *chi* in Tai Chi. Aries is the art of meeting the living moment, as if each moment has something for you that you can't retrieve unless you dive in. So many vital connections would die on the vine if this most eager member of the zodiac didn't dive.

Throughout our lives, destiny asks us to dance, but we shake it off, caught in whatever agenda happens to be running our minds that moment. If I'd clung to Santa Cruz after all the losses I would've probably kept spinning my wheels. Hopping into the saddle sprang me from the dead to the living, though it would eventually take another year or so after Sedona for the numbness to wear off.

Inside the most pragmatic ram a romantic lurks beneath a blue-and-white striped awning, awaiting a rendezvous beside the cut-glass vase of fresh flowers sitting on a cafe table. Like Paris in the 1920s, a part of every Aries wants to stay awake all night long exchanging food, sex and conversation.

The Aries experience changes radically when love comes along. Similar to how the sign dives into a moment, it tends to dive into relationship, which can work well if the pool is deep and the person ready. If not, due to its straightforward approach this isn't the best sign to sort subtle agendas and mixed messages. Those kinds of love often lock horns with Aries like bighorn rams in mating season.

Since I launched my astrology career in 1987, fewer Aries clients have come to me than any other sign. I think this is because the most self-directed member of the zodiac is less likely to make themselves dependent on the counsel of others, and perhaps less inclined to follow metaphysics in general, which can seem far removed from the shortest distance between two points. When Aries does get interested in the subtle arts, though, they tend to go very far very fast.

After Aries gets the ball rolling, the vast majority of the zodiac is yet to come, which is why it's not up to the introductory sign to make sure everything's neatly tied with no loose ends. But it *is* up to Aries to get things off to a good start, and though this is largely a matter of intention, it's also a matter of *energy*.

The secret superpower of the first sign is the use of energy. The kind of energy I mean makes a cat run up to one stranger and turn tail on another. Cats are so masterful at reading and running energy they can lie down on a king-sized bed with two humans in it, and somehow confine the big bodies to a cramped little margin. Many animals are energy experts and so are young children. Adults, not so much, because we get clogged with excess thought, jaded by experience and sidetracked by ego, and childhood's psychic feelers dull from lack of use.

One night a couple of years before he turned my crises toward harvest, I went with my Aries friend Scott to a party at a farmhouse on the outskirts of Santa Cruz. Following him three steps in from the door, I saw his eyes dart birdlike left, right and center, where he asked the hostess, "Did something big just happen here?"

"*Yeah*—my neighbor just called the cops and about a hundred people left."

Scott nodded, as if confirming something he already knew.

Somehow he'd read invisible vapor trails I'd been oblivious to. Like the wake of an ocean liner after the ship passed, he must've sensed energy currents that parted when the guests rushed off.

If you follow energy through the world like dowsing, functions previously assigned to your analytical process shift to direct. En route to Prescott, if I hadn't gotten so hot under the collar, if I'd paused coolly at each intersection to analyze which way to go, I might not have gotten there.

In our information-heavy, instinct-weak period of history, the Aries part of us craves direct encounter. Below the pixelated deluge of noninformation, we long to break out of delayed gratification into something fresh, vital and alive.

In the end it turns out what this sign has been seeking is just what it started with, except more: more direct connection, more ecstatic release, more satisfying moments, more rich exchange of energies, like electricity that keeps steadily flowing.

Like the Zen master brandishing his bowl to the thief, and like Francis rushing out of his father's market stall to dwell among the wild creatures on the mountain, even a complex modern life, if you're ready to release its clutter, can be stripped down, enabling you to move through the world like a finger pointing at the moon.

.

ARIES DRAGONHEAD/LIBRA DRAGONTAIL

From the complicated to the simple

With Libra behind you and Aries ahead, you're departing from the complicated and heading toward the simple. Beware second-guessing. Trust your gut. Pondering comes naturally to you because you got good at it in an earlier life, but don't linger there, or you'll stumble around a clockface of past-life footprints. Direct engagement is what you came back for. You have to engage more than your mind, though, and dive off the clock into strong subtle energies that usher you forward. That dive streamlines your ride through the physical plane, bypassing convoluted thought webs that trap the free movement of individuals. As quick as thought travels, energy travels quicker. Underneath the complexities of our time, the spirit of the species is fuming to bust loose, and Aries leads the charge. Thoughts can carry human consciousness into the future, but energy links your subtle senses to life-enhancing forces of the present. Your dragon is stalking evolutionary breakthroughs you might not find with your mind, but they can be identified by the tingling in the forearms of the dowser in you.

From
the simple to the
complicated

ARIES DRAGONTAIL/LIBRA DRAGONHEAD

With Aries behind you and Libra ahead, you're departing from the simple and heading toward the complicated. In earlier lives you saw most things entirely through your own eyes while missing the views of others. You got so caught up in your own track you couldn't tell if it was veering toward or away from someone else's, which limited your empathy and understanding. This time around you're developing clairsentience, which, similar to clairvoyance (which is psychic vision) and clairaudience (psychic hearing), enables you to sense what others are experiencing without needing to be told. The more you care about someone, the sharper this sense grows. It takes lots of back-and-forth to master it. Going too far can unbalance you by becoming so inundated with the other person's experience you lose track of your own. Not going far enough risks chasing your tail by repeating past-life self-enclosure. Your dragon is flying out of a narrow past toward the shared world that manifests when two get together heart to heart and soul to soul. If you're in one of those shared worlds, put your ear to the ground and learn to listen. If you're not and want to be, put your ear to the ground and listen anyway, because that world is busy being born in you the same time it's being born in the person you're going to share it with as soon as you're both ready to find each other.

CHAPTER TWO

Just as spring's warmth follows winter's chill, an aura of promise seems to follow Taurus around. And just as a bucolic panorama of cows on a hillside suggests contentment, the presence of this springtime sign can feel reassuring, suggesting that even though life on Earth has become strange these days, some things, at least, can still be counted on.

Their ability to recognize quality and grasp the way things operate draws this resourceful sign into situations where others depend on them. They're often viewed as rock-solid, but, like a calf on spindly legs, their own experience is usually a bit shakier than that. Perhaps their inherent understanding of quality makes them very aware of things that fall short of what they could be, and uneasy about whether they should do something about it.

Thoughtful more than impulsive, Taurus is the hands-on inventive engineer of the zodiac, who loves to get its hands on ideas, tools, instruments and other things that adjust, tighten or just plain feel good to touch (which leads to Taurean sex, which I'll get to in a moment).

An abundance of tactile awareness seems to give Taureans the sense of life as something to grasp and hold. When things go that way, Taurus is a happy camper, but grumbly and out of sorts when it doesn't, though many of the sign's biggest lessons are provoked by such anomalies the way a bull is provoked by a matador's flashing cape.

I see Taurus as the gardener of the zodiac, in a garden of possibilities.

Now that Aries got the ball rolling, it's up to Taurus to figure out what to do with it. Now that the first sign launched the journey of individuation, the second contemplates how best to use it.

How to use and be used comprise the large part of bovine journeys. Most Taureans spend their lives looking for a way to be used that nourishes the body and satisfies the soul, but they have to spend a lot of time getting used for the wrong reasons before they find it.

Though they're one of the most industrious signs, most Taureans delight in puttering around, peeking in on what the wind and weather are up to in the garden, or doing nothing at all. As with a cow chewing its cud, or a gardener kneeling on the ground, the bulk of Taurine attention is often directed down and in rather than up and out.

One of Taurus's fondest notions—which the universe seems hell-bent on sabotaging—is to contemplate its life away. What action is to the first sign, stillness is to the second, rich contemplative stillness, where seeds germinate in darkness far from the busyness.

A Garden of Possibilities: The Taurus Art of Essence

As MUCH AS IT DELIGHTS IN PUTTERING AROUND, TAURUS is also one of the most motivated signs, and intelligent enough to realize that not every possibility will fulfill its potential. Which means the efficacy of its groundskeeping can't be ensured, but coaxed by a compost of steady nurturing and elbow grease.

At least half the Taurine experience is wrapped up in contemplation and waiting, because plants can't be forced to grow. All possibilities can't be indulged with the same consummate devotion. And even if they are, some will invariably wilt.

But strong decisive action is the all-important other half of the Taurus experience, which often gets forestalled by its tendency to procrastinate. The amount of repeat thinking Taurus lavishes on pet ideas wears grooves into the universe that can swallow cows whole, which sometimes leaves direct action as the only way out of the ditch.

When trying to square their actions with their thoughts, and vice versa, if they get interrupted, Taureans can feel *in flagrante delicto,* which could be hazardous if too much *thoughtus interruptus* turns a shy bovine into a raging bull.

Though most Tauruses have a rational disposition and are slow to anger, it'd be a mistake to assume they're not paying attention or don't care. Regarding what they hold dear, caring runs deep for this largely affable but fiercely loyal sign.

Unlike some signs, sexuality for Taurus seems more mandatory than optional. Though many go long periods without, I think they're sitting on a smoldering volcano. Similar to Taurus's earth-sign cousins, Virgo and Capricorn, their wellbeing often seems more physiologically based than psychologically, and I feel the source of much earth-sign misery is trapped passion.

Values, sex and money fall within the domain of the second sign, and when I was a young astrologer I puzzled over their common denominator, other than these are all good things to get your hands on. Money can obviously be linked with values, but how does sex fit with values? And, apart from prostitution, why would money go with sex?

Eventually I realized that what you spend money on and who you spend sex with are statements of worth. Both are methods of intercourse intended to supply something satisfying for their investment. Both predominate in power struggles, office politics and gender wars. Both are so fundamental to the human experience it's likely that at any given moment most people over the age of fifteen are thinking about one or the other. Each can be used for leverage and coercion as well as acts of generosity and caring.

If you earn money doing something that feeds the soul, the taking in and giving out of those funds may transfer more than their numerical value. Similar to *prasad* in a Hindu *kirtan* (food offerings placed on the altar before ceremonially singing the names of God), the money may be thought of as absorbing sacred vibrations that are distributed when you distribute the funds.

If you make love in a way that feeds the soul, those vibes can also get transferred. Lately I've been imagining an afterglow that lasts the rest of my life, and occasionally think I may be getting close.

Lack of money is usually easier for this sign to deal with than lack of sex. Money seems to be the commodity most Taureans, after a bit of fussing and deliberation, can switch on at will, as if from a mystic spigot in the garden. But sex is woven through a more complex root system.

Lovers who try to grow their sexuality sometimes get directed toward exotic positions, trendy gadgets or multiple partners, but the source of sexuality runs deeper than that. It can be unlocked by approaching your lover each time you approach as a luscious garden you're about to enter for the first time.

Lack of sex can frustrate Taureans, but lack of deeply fulfilling sex may be more frustrating, since it's harder to diagnose. Because Taurus, similar to neighbor Aries, is one of the most basic, hardy and independent signs, it's not easy to tell when they're suffering.

But when a Taurus suffers, the cause is rarely hard to find. Apart from sex, the care and feeding of this sign depend on three primal elements as non-negotiable as soil, water and sun.

The sun that makes Taurus grow is the strong clear light of sustained creative purpose. When it's lacking, Taurus withers. When it's present, that's almost all this sign needs.

The cleansing water of clear feelings, which it's freely able to either hold onto or express as need be, is the second basic.

Taurus is a self-sufficient sign who tends to keep a lot of things at bay. After Aries championed the direct approach, it's natural for bovines to hang back and chew their cud. But as long as Taurus is feeling its feelings rather than living at a distance from them, it's got number two out of three.

The rich soil of a life that feels good and works right is the third primal element, which may be the most elusive, because a life that feels good and works right is very different than a life that sort of feels good or kind of works right. Due to their tendency to stiffen under pressure, lock in track and trudge like an ox, it can take Taureans a while to tell the difference.

The sun of creative purpose, watered by the springs of feeling your feelings, rooted in the soil of a meaningful existence, would likely produce the best in anyone, but for Taurus can be downright orgasmic. If you add in sumptuous food and sex, you'll see bulls doing backflips in Bovine Nirvana.

When Taurus lacks one, two, or all three of these elements, its life force can get frittered away on barren soil. After a while its green thumb (not necessarily for plants but for growing *something*) reverts to flesh color.

As one of the earliest and therefore most fundamental signs, when Taurus loses basic functionality it's hard for it to compensate. Unlike more cosmic and expansive signs further down the zodiac, bovines usually require something basic and graspable to make their way back to the garden.

Taurus is quality, values and meaning. In recent decades, as superficial values took over society, meaning went missing. The Taurus in each of us has the best shot at bringing it back. When this sign rolls up its sleeves, the universe takes notice.

This is where the inventive genius of the sign comes in, because among the forms needed to regenerate meaning in today's world, some may not have been invented yet, but like necessity, Taurus is the mother of invention.

Even those rare Taureans inept with tools, instruments or plants often possess a green thumb for bringing nonmaterial things to life, like Freud, a Taurus who dug deep enough in the garden of possibilities to raise a blueprint for the human psyche.

Like Freudian analysis, infamous for taking forever to unearth rich bottomlands of meaning hidden beneath cover stories of ego, Taurus's quest for essence and the forms to serve it can lead down many garden paths before bearing fruit. Even during a time of distorted values, essence is always there, somewhere; but like a tender seedling in an overgrown garden, it can use a lot of help to blossom.

In an ideal world, essence and form would make a fine marriage. Source and format, meaning and method, would be each other's perfect mates, with a life path arising naturally from the wholeness within you. Parents and peers would recognize a child's essence from the get-go and lavish their attention on it, rather than rewarding it for fitting into the Machine.

In today's world, form and essence have gotten divorced, planting many lives in barren soil. Each day millions go about an existence that has nothing to do with who they are.

Halfway down the zodiac, when we enter the lair of the scorpion, we'll delve into the cost of those kinds of lives. But here at this more innocent stage, the sign with hungry hands must gain a firm handle on the life it loves rather than the one it settles for—if it wants to fully blossom.

Most Taureans take a while to bloom and spend much of their life restraining their impulses. That kind of restraint can build inner strength, but too much holding back can lame a bovine until it learns the difference between self-negation and self-restraint.

Self-restraint comes naturally to this sign, who's more concerned with securing the value of life than tooting its own horn.

Self-negation has to do with getting turned against yourself on a primal level, which can poison the garden.

Taureans often gets consumed working some patch of soil without putting their heart and soul in, because they may be stretched thin and because other things get in the way. Many Taureans make a cottage industry of coping strategies, which postpone releasing the immense strength packed into them.

If they ever release it, the devotion of a Brahma Bull will very likely take it anywhere it wants to go. Hesitation about inappropriately throwing their weight around may result from the part of them that knows how strong they are and is leery of having to handle that much power.

Taurus is built to improve things and bring out quality, but the complex machinery of today's world may be difficult to improve upon without first dismantling it.

There seems to be a peculiar bugaboo of our time, which makes few things we do complete in and of themselves, without spawning another thing that needs doing, which spawns another, and another—the bane of a sign bent on quality.

Sooner or later some Taureans realize that as they move through the world they've been parading a telepathic sandwich board that says:

USE ME

Taurus's proclivity to fix and sustain can backfire when it prevents others from growing independently capable. Because of their need to be needed, it may take repeated interventions to awaken Taureans to the revelation that just because they can fix things better than others, that doesn't mean they have to.

Few things feel as sublime to a Taurus as being used for the right reasons, and few feel as awful as being wrongly used, though that's where much of their growth takes place.

Many Taureans delight in learning the laws of how things operate, so they can bend those laws and seduce reality to go how they want it to go, though a natural bovine shyness makes them slow to claim credit.

Like organic gardening, which, unlike factory farming, leaves the soil more renewed after harvest than before, sustainability is an idea that compels much Taurine thought.

When the second sign finds a sustainable and replenishing way to live, you'll find no more contented being: cow on a hillside, implacable, rising above the earth like a big fat Buddha, in the world but not of it.

Their garden nature lends some Taureans a dreamy quality that others may find inspirational or off-putting, depending on what they want from Taurus. However intimate this sign becomes with others, every Taurus needs uncluttered mental space to chew on, and plenty of time to digest with those four stomachs.

Perhaps more than any other corrective for getting off-kilter, the richness of solitude works wonders for Taurus. Which indicates the greatest treasures of this most materialistic sign are not material at all, but gifts of essence: Time apart. Shelter. Renewal. Time off. Time away…. Such gifts allow Taurus to sink into the luxurious contemplation most Taureans only dream of.

Lacking the orchard of sacred space, its eagerness to make good on projects can run this sign ragged. Laboring like a yoked ox, Tauruses can plow along full steam ahead until waking up one day far from the garden. The return path has less to do with putting nose back to the grindstone than with entering the silence.

The silence of Taurus is one of the most profound in the zodiac. It seems to post a notice on the garden gate:

> I'll be back in a moment to resume affairs. Meanwhile, despite what anybody else thinks or wants, before I make my next move I'm sounding the depths to learn whether I'm about to leave an indispensable part of myself behind. Check back with me in a minute, or maybe another lifetime.

A bull's great strength can work against it when it fails to honor its sovereignty and preserve its sacred space.

Relationships prosper when the independent sovereignty of each person flourishes. Time apart, if only for an hour now and then, but often for far more, is crucial to cleanse Taurean palates and restore their connection to source.

Nature, in its sun-drenched or rain-soaked glory, can be a most powerful restorative. Sex can go either way, becoming a source of conflict or replenishment, depending on the state of the relationship, but for such an earthy sign there are moments when nothing else will suffice.

Like the reassuring presence of a cow in a field, Taurus's contributions often occur so unobtrusively they're easy to miss. This by itself isn't usually a sore point with the second sign, who rarely possesses the dominant ego of other signs (Taureans tend to step into the spotlight more reluctantly than wholeheartedly). But it becomes an issue if it causes them to undervalue themselves.

Taurus is the quality of *quality,* as dependable as a weathered hand on a pump handle, drawing life-giving nutrients from below the ground. Pride in craft, common in earlier ages but rare in much of the world nowadays, is key to Taurean happiness. If all else fails, the ability to make something (by hand or mind) can reopen the garden gate.

Acutely aware of the susceptibility of human nature to falter when things get shaky, the Taurine default is to bear down and adjust all kinds of components that may or may not need adjusting.

Though not usually an egotistical sign, Taurus can be controlling, which may result from a compulsion to do something—*anything*—to combat dysfunction and raise quality. However, such exertion may also result from the gardener's and engineer's sensing where the life force of a person or machine wants to go next for optimal growth.

Consumed by the urge to handle tasks impeccably, because anything less leaves them with a pang of lost opportunity (and Taurus is allergic to wastefulness), the zodiac's gardener may fail to recognize when incessant fussing endangers the plants.

There comes a point in the Taurus journey when, even though things could still be improved, the drastic maneuver of letting go must be executed. Though the quality controller still has itchy fingers, surrender and release are required, confronting the most hands-on sign with the need to take its hands off.

Taurus is the fidelity between who you are and how you live, which in today's world can take a long time to synchronize. Few of us were taught the value of being true to ourselves as much as we were taught the value of fitting in with others.

In a perfect garden, society would beam into children the message:

> **You didn't come here to make anyone else happy. You came to learn the truth of your soul and follow it through the world. We don't care if you marry a man, woman, white, black, Jew, Hindu, or nobody. We don't care if you gain a million admirers or a million dollars. We don't care how long it takes. We only care that you find your truth and never stop following it. Trust what you know in your heart, and beware anyone who tries to talk you out of it.**

In our world few of us were raised so pristinely, and often have to discover essence and learn to value and protect it on our own, or with the help of others later in life. Sometimes very late.

As one of the simplest signs, Taurus doesn't need much: time to ruminate, room to stretch out and clean air to breathe. Food. Massage. The sun of creative purpose, the clear flow of feelings, and the soil of a life that feels good and works right. Great food and sex now and then would be nice.

Such basic happiness should be the birthright of us all rather than a rare attainment. There's something mighty peculiar about a planet full of people running around doing things that have little to do with who they are. But many of those forms are breaking down to compost and the world is changing. The Taurus in each of us is primed to invent new methods for tending the garden. Life doesn't necessarily become easy, but it becomes *real* when you live from essence.

TAURUS DRAGONHEAD/SCORPIO DRAGONTAIL

From obsession to innocence

With Scorpio behind you and Taurus ahead, you're departing from obsession and heading toward innocence. Your soul's been scurrying like a scorpion through reincarnational tunnels that demanded obsession with the basics and little room for anything else. Such rawness gave you x-ray vision, supercharged your survival instincts and revealed skeletons in many closets. Despite all that, you've come back to swing on lamp posts and dance jigs in mausoleums. Your willingness to emerge from the karmic tunnel is being sorely tested, summoning you to gain a faith that moves mountains. When you're aware of the odds against love prevailing and bet everything on it anyway, your dragon digs deep into the garden of life with an innocence that can make the sun rise. It's easy for the naive among us to be innocent, but you signed up for something harder: a chance for the veteran soul to become young again, not by being gullible and easily duped, but by resurrecting a sense of wonder so deep it can't be denied.

From innocence to obsession

TAURUS DRAGONTAIL/SCORPIO DRAGONHEAD

With Taurus behind you and Scorpio ahead, you're departing from innocence and heading toward obsession. The purity of childhood holds a dear place in your heart, as a fond refuge that beckons when invasive forces intrude. But beyond that shelter your dragon is calling, and its way is rough and raw but realer than every other. You were born to claim truths that can't be won by concession and compromise. If someone tells you to tame down, you're too intense, too obsessed, too *much,* they're correct— you're far too much for everything that's not enough, but exactly right to dig your claws into the farce that has turned a planetful of dragons into herd animals. You're a warrior of love who's not here to tippytoe through social niceties, but to fan your wings whipping up a wind that sweeps the underworld clean. Depending on your chosen field, you may or may not wish to draw attention to this, but operate undercover like a spiritual outlaw, stealing complacency and replacing it with passion. Like a scorpion or dragon, you'll have to molt every so often, so don't get too attached to anything but love.

CHAPTER THREE

Picture a house with no floors, doors, walls, roof, ceilings or windows, and you'll begin to get an idea of where Gemini lives, though they spend so much time galivanting around the universe, stretching the fabric of existence every which way, that you're not likely to find the twins home any time soon if you come calling; and besides, as one of the zodiac's premier shapeshifters, how would you know if you did?

If the prior paragraph intrigues and perplexes more than clarifies, Congratulations! You've just entered the paradoxical, metamorphic, M.C. Escher-like realm of the twins (Escher was a Gemini), where— you'll be relieved to know as you climb those marvelous staircases leading down and descend the ones going up—you only have to dwell for the length of a single chapter rather than your whole life. (Unless you're a Gemini, in which case you have my sympathies, because the only reason you would've reincarnated as a twin would be if your past lives had been so contained and predictable that to restore karmic balance in this life you have to toss everything up in the air and scramble around putting it back together again several times a day. Before breakfast.)

If this sounds crazy-making that's because it often is, but a Gemini life, like every other, gains a method to its madness when you grasp the missing piece of how it emerges from its past-life history, rather than viewing it as an isolated event that has no continuity with what came before.

The history of your soul is the old foundation you came back to build something new on. You reincarnated to bring the strengths of your past lives forward while leaving their limitations behind. Those reincarnational themes have a way of returning in many variations throughout your life.

Even though most of us don't know who we were in previous lives, the clues to that mystery, as Sherlock Holmes might say, are hidden in plain sight, where business you previously handled well produces an ease of passage in certain areas, while in other areas unfinished business clouds your aspirations and overcasts your fresh starts.

If you cloud up each time you approach certain areas like sex, self-love, creativity, health or money, you may be experiencing time leakage at a karmic crossroads, where the present is in danger of getting run over by the past.

Such intersections summon you to learn the difference between soul and ego, which is often what Gemini is trying to do underneath everything else it's trying to do.

Probably the most underestimated sign, every twin has infinitely more to them than meets the eye, but also so much that does meet the eye that between the parts of Gemini you see and the parts you don't, you're bound to get befuddled as to what this sign's all about. Getting befuddled, however, is a good first step toward understanding Gemini, who, perhaps more than any other sign, spends much time in that state.

Don't be fooled, though: even befuddled, Gemini is ingeniously capable and has a stunningly vast reach, though it may take numerous perambulations for Geminis to wake up to this, and even longer for those around Gemini.

The extremes of this sign often provoke a twin to run before it walks and fly before it runs, which means a lot of Geminis chase themselves around the universe a few lifetimes before catching up. Most nights you can catch them down at the crossroads with their thumb up, hitching a ride.

Satori at the Crossroads: The Gemini Art of Being Two Places at Once

CROSSROADS WERE SACRED TO HERMES, PATRON SAINT OF thieves and travelers (and Geminis), where the unfinished business of the past and bright promise of the future intertwine around your current location like twin serpents wrapped around the winged wand of Hermes, better known as the caduceus, which stands for the freedom you gain when you make peace with the past and release its long shadow.

Unlike next-door neighbor Taurus, and more similar to the sign two doors down, Aries, Gemini is less fixated on digging down than moving on. But even if you're as freewheeling as the third sign, before you embark on your great adventure you still might wish to go back in the kitchen to see if you left a burner on.

From the viewpoint of less restless signs (which is almost all of them), Gemini's fast change-ups and frequent-flyer miles may look like fickle escapism (which they may in fact be), but in light of the logjam that has stalled society at the current crossroads of history, Gemini may be our best hope.

Always a changer, often a trickster, definitely a thief who steals ideas from one part of the universe to stash them in another, the third sign inherits the linear momentum of Aries and urgency of Taurus, but with less pressure than either, because now that the journey has made it to the crucial third step, like a pregnancy in the third trimester it's out of immediate danger and can relax.

The first two signs launched the journey and got it on track. However, they weren't built to take much time off until the hardiness of the quest was ensured. But Aries is so good at launching energies and Taurus so stellar at staying on track, there's little now to keep Gemini from opening the throttle.

Though this sign is often ambiguous and elusive (not to mention exasperating), it holds the key to the human future, because our species has gotten terribly stuck and Gemini is wondrously unstuck. (Except when it isn't, as we'll see when we venture deeper into the House of Escher.)

Transistasis is the ability of living things to change in accord with changing circumstances. Homeostasis is the tendency for living things to hold steady within pre-arranged limits. Which means we all have the ability to evolve and the determination not to—forces that clash inside each of us, and clash even more in collective consciousness, which is having the damnedest time trying to outgrow its shadow.

The idea of treating others the way you wish to be treated is not new. It's at the root of world religion, though we don't appear to have gotten much better at following it since the days of Cain and Abel, and unless we depolarize this ancient split there's little chance for our species to have a future.

If you're a Gemini, you signed up to wrestle with duality, but once in that wrestling ring it's hard to get out, until you get knocked out by the truth that every dogmatic belief unwittingly perpetuates its opposite, and you can't dehumanize anyone without doing the same to yourself.

An intermediate step to transcend polarization is to shift from unconsciously polarizing to polarizing consciously, so you can learn duality's lessons and crack its codes before fully getting out.

Gemini's satori at the crossroads is that you *can* be in two places at once. You can work duality creatively, imaginatively, shamanically, as Karmic Theatre, rather than taking it literally. Like a rabid New York Yankees fan who's convinced the Yankees rule and Red Sox are the scum of the Earth, who falls in love with a Red Sox fan and moves to Boston, drops acid and has a change of heart, we need creative ways to work polarity till we make it to the other side.

As many Beatle biographies and film clips mention, Gemini Paul McCartney practiced conscious dualism during the heyday of Beatlemania by psychologically splitting himself into *World Famous Beatle* and *Just Plain Paul*. Just Plain Paul is as much in awe of the Beatles as is anyone. Probably more so. The fact that his childhood home is on the historic register and he's royal blows the mind of *Just Plain Paul,* who, like a biological twin, is telepathically bonded with his more famous sibling but is having his own completely independent experience. This creative bifurcation, which I've heard Paul ascribe to being a Gemini, kept the Mac sane during the deluge.

Compared to the relative simplicity of the first two signs, this is complex territory. In Gemini, Aries's eagerness to surge forward and Taurus's inclination to hold steady vie for supremacy in a contest that bashes this sign around like a tether ball.

Gaining attention is a game this game-loving sign excels at, but some graduate to the more interesting game of finding out who they are, which for Gemini can produce identity crisis as a kind of life art. This makes sense when you consider it the sign of friends and neighbors, then look at the company it keeps.

As the first human in the line-up, following a sheep and a cow, and preceding a crab and a lion, Gemini is an upright hominid surrounded by three four-legged mammals and one ten-legged crustacean: How can this not be strange?

After Aries kicks off the twelve-stage journey, and Taurus gets down and gritty with it, the twins hit town like acrobats in a traveling circus, spending half their time exclaiming, *Wheee look at me!* and the other half protesting, *Don't look at me—I didn't have anything to do with this!* By the time you figure out who to look at, the spotlight is cold, the tents are down and the circus is gone.

Such vacillation can make Gemini the hope of the world or the bane of one's existence—often both, since most things twins partake of involve duality and, like Russian nesting dolls, each duality might contain a duality.

To give itself a break from constant movement, it's tempting for Gemini to latch onto any port in the storm. But premature mooring can be worse than none; just when you think you're anchored and base your plans on it, you find yourself adrift and have to start over.

Contrarily, if Gemini waits *too* long to ground into something definitive, freedom can become its own prison, like a treadmill of starts that don't go anywhere. Amidst such changes of motion this sign's breezy casualness and quick retorts often belie the intensity of its inner process, where it's striving to get free of self-doubt and awaken from escapist illusion.

But even through diversions galore, a Gemini life, like an Escher lithograph, is made of unfathomable perspectives that become can openers that pop the lid of the universe when you open your mind.

Perhaps due to having gotten stuck in past lives, Gemini is hyper-alert to the games people play. They sometimes cleverly avoid the games of others for years only to get caught in games of their own. And so it is with each of us: Our disguises have disguises, which can both reveal and conceal.

One of the third sign's favorite games is *Earnest Searcher versus Mischievous Provoker.*

Mischievous Provoker pushes buttons to see what happens. *Earnest Searcher* seeks revelations it can share, because even though Gemini frequently talks up a blue streak, which may wrap around and around its own ideas, it shines like the sun in like-minded company, approaching intriguing concepts like a wine-taster picking up a stem glass.

But when the *Provoker* grabs the spotlight, it's hard to tell the substance of what it's saying from what it's acting out for effect. Often Geminis themselves can't tell; they juggle so many ideas it's easy for them to get lost in the junkyard of the mind.

When playing *Provoker,* many things Gemini says should be taken with a grain of salt. Like a precocious teenager, this one gets kicks triggering others, and any rebuttal someone offers is likely to add fuel to the fire. Best grant this side of Gemini a wide berth for acting out the melodrama of the moment, rather than risk becoming the latest casualty of the Polarity Wars.

Despite their penchant for provocation, Gemini dramas often contain redeeming elements. Acting out might show Gemini what others are made of by dint of their response. And like echolocation, firing off provocative statements can enable a twin to monitor its underlying truth by measuring how those statements feel when they bounce back. For these reasons, annoying as it may be, provoking others might show Gemini what it's made of, one of the great unsolved mysteries of the zodiac no one seems to get to the bottom of.

But because most of what the *Provoker* does is designed for effect, it can polarize the space until well-meaning cohorts are faced with the unenviable choice of ignoring the provoker or re-provoking it, neither of which is likely to foster the meeting of hearts and minds Gemini is really after. Vacillations between *Earnest Searcher* and *Mischievous Provoker* can become so extreme it's hard to take either seriously.

Even though it pings around the universe at the speed of light, Gemini thought is often surprisingly lucid and directly on target. However, Gemini logic sometimes lacks compassion and can be insensitive.

But if its heart opens even half as much as its mind, this sign can be a most delightful companion. Few signs are as fun to be with or as quick to expand the playground of shared ideas.

For its ideas to be taken seriously, skilled communication is needed, but Gemini communication has a way of getting wonky, producing a love/hate relationship with words, which some Geminis learn to treat as dubious critters that turn and snap with no warning.

Taurus Joan Baez addressed this wonkiness in her public love letter to her ex, Gemini Bob Dylan, the song "Diamonds and Rust":

...Now you're telling me
You're not nostalgic
Then give me another word for it

You who are so good with words
And at keeping things vague...

'Cause I need some of that vagueness now
It's all come back too clearly
Yes, I loved you dearly
And if you're offering me diamonds and rust
I've already paid...

© 1975 Chandos Music Company, USA

More than anyone I know of, Dylan adopted different voices throughout his career. And his penchant for changing keys, tempos, rhythms, time signatures and lyrics, of even his best-known songs, at the last minute, when the mood suited him, kept bandmates on their toes.

Whether such shapeshifting is the mark of awesome genius or slippery escapism is a question best answered *Yes*. Between the one and the other, many Gemini lives exhibit the cosmic irony of the Yiddish proverb that says the best way to make God laugh is to tell him your plans.

A good way to draw the real Gemini out is through humor. Most twins are sufficiently skewed to appreciate absurdity around them, and Gemini laughter ripples freely like a brook and is highly contagious.

Growing up with an older Gemini sister, one of my favorite things to do was improvise ongoing narratives that bent our family experiences into a twisted sitcom that made us laugh so hard we cried. When Gemini laughs at the human condition but takes its lessons to heart, it gains skill at being two places at once.

Most twins learn early in the game that life is made of games, and somewhere along the line some of them begin to wonder if there's a better game, a game so good they never have to stop playing.

Superficial games Gemini plays with itself and others, like old tv shows, get boring fast. Probably more than any other sign, twins languish when caught in repetition and thrive while innovating, which can make them exhilarating but exhausting to be around. But not even the most progressive Gemini can only break new trails without ever doubling back.

Looking back over their footsteps, some twins realize many of their evasive tactics were unwittingly designed to capture their own attention: *It was myself all along I was trying to impress....*

And though they may have only a fleeting glimpse of what that self is, they come closer when they stop rebounding off others to figure it out, and look within. That can be the game-changer which takes a lot of games to get to.

If you want to uncover the final Matryoshka doll, you can shadow a twin by accompanying its rounds as it goes about ticking chores off the outrageous list of things it planned to accomplish that day.

Somewhere in the wee hours it may dawn on Gemini that it's not going to come close to completing the list and might as well resort to the drastic, last-ditch, seldom-attempted, daredevil Gemini recourse of being itself.

During such raw moments of unguarded exposure, when the Escher stairways come down and Russian dolls lay disassembled, an intoxicating sweetness often arises from this sign, accompanied by the deepening of its presence and softening of its voice. If I were going to ask a twin to marry me, that's when I'd do it.

Though twins are frequently surrounded by others, have lots of friends and keep company with diverse personality types, they often suffer a camouflaged form of loneliness hard to spot within their bustling activity. If that melancholy sinks into chronic depression, it's probably because Gemini succumbed to one or both of the following assumptions:

1. Everything in the world worth knowing has already been figured out.
2. Nothing significant is likely to change.

This is dangerous territory. Either belief could hobble any sign, but the combo is particularly deadly for the Dioscuri (the mythological twins who symbolize Gemini), because when this youthful and eager sign gets jaded, its doppelganger can't be far behind: the dark double who steals its identity. Regardless of Sun sign, we all have dark doubles who move in at key karmic crunches.

You may have crossed paths with a doppelganger one day when you started out clear and bright, then got ambushed by someone's shadow-self who was busy firing tennis balls (or basketballs) (or *bowling* balls) of toxic negativity over the net, and despite your best intentions, before long you found yourself not lobbing them but *smashing* them back.

In the realm of the dark twin, as if possessed, two people who care about each other get evicted from their relationship as their shadow-selves take over. Sometimes a doppel lies dormant for years until a cross word or provocative statement triggers its reemergence and *bam,* out come the cannonballs.

However twisted shadow twins get, the cure has more to do with raw presence and open-hearted vulnerability than with rationalizations and justifications, which this sign often gets lost in.

It's hard to win a quarrel with a Gemini because it's used to arguing both sides of every issue. The visionary musician Van Morrison (a Virgo) suggests an antidote for this kind of polarization in his song "I Forgot That Love Existed":

> If my heart could do the thinking
> And my head begin to feel
> I would look upon the world anew
> And know what's truly real...

© 1987 Van Morrison, BMG Rights Management

Which leads to Gemini love. When love blossoms in the house with no walls, walls may spring up, because all the magnificent aspirations Gemini has been skating around get aimed at somebody who's aiming whatever *they've* been skating around at Gemini. And twinning a twin who twins a twin is like holding a lit stick of dynamite while cartwheeling through a hall of mirrors.

Such confrontations can produce long-overdue soul searching for a sign whose mental life is robust, but emotional life can be shaky. Gemini is so geared to take things in stride and continue on its merry way that learning to hold steady and see itself through the eyes of an intimate other can launch a medicine journey of staggering proportions.

Once it opens the doors of its heart, though, most Geminis will be reluctant to close them, because one of the sign's fondest wishes is for a running mate to explore the universe with. Finding one can transport Gemini to cloud nine, but also sober up a sign who spends a lot of time brainstorming ways to preserve its freedom.

When you're accustomed to flying carpets and nesting dolls, the idea of showing up naked with blemishes exposed in front of another human being can be the most terrifying of all. Movement, change and adventure rarely intimidate this sign as much as confrontation.

When feeling trapped, Gemini may seize upon the slightest clue its partner is not who they appear to be, and bolt. If you partner a Gemini, tread lightly, because once misled—even if it's an imaginary transgression—a twin can jump ship with no warning and never look back. Suspicion of getting tricked by someone being other than they appear can inflame the sign who spends much time trying to determine which, if any, of its own self-portrayals is real.

On one hand, this sign needs broad latitude to indulge its freedom, or may grow resentful. On the other, Gemini craves companionship, which requires intimacy, which requires trust, so a lover who looks the other way *too* much may strike Gemini as a weak container for all it yearns to share.

It takes a canny paramour to sense how to *come in* and *stay out* far enough to provide intimacy while granting freedom. But it can be more than worth it, because Gemini offers an abundance of gifts for anyone bold enough to take up residence in the House of Escher.

Falling in love with a Gemini is like polyamory without risk of STDs. Gemini conversations alone can be near-orgasmic—rarely can two people have as much fun without lying down.

This sign needs to be wooed from many different angles, so if one fails, try another. As with a shy animal, sudden moves are likely to backfire, but charm and humor go far, and few Geminis can resist flattery—especially when it's real (the best kind).

Twins urgently crave and fear commitment, so timing is of the essence. If you advance too soon they may bolt, but if you delay too long they may lose interest.

Though it can take quite some doing for Gemini to open its heart, that's the only way it will gain the thing most twins are looking for—self-trust, which is the final Matryoshka doll.

When Gemini hearts open it's hard to keep anybody's closed, because this sign's enthusiasm is catching. And if magic strikes, and hearts twin in radical intimacy, the universe might open, as was written in ancient days:

> Beyond ideas of right and wrong there is a field.
> I will meet you there,

says Rumi, opening a door to mystical union beyond duality.

Perhaps some dualities are built into the universe and will never change, like the division of the genders that procreates life on Earth, or twin stars that orbit each other in deep space, or mourning doves, who mate for life.

Four and a half billion years ago, a small planetary body smashed into the newborn Earth, tilting our axis (which created the seasons) and ejecting a chunk out of the opposite side of the world, which flew into orbit and became the moon.

Earth and moon are the two who used to be one. And so it is with each of us, as we go about searching for our missing piece.

The trickster and the thief approached the crossroads the same time the cop and the saint approached from the other side, and all found out they're reflections of each other.

Or—the trickster and the thief approached the crossroads the same time as the cop and the saint, and all found out they're being drawn by the hand of Escher, who himself is being drawn by deserters from the Polarity Wars, who threw down their weapons and picked up their paints.

To be willing and eager in a universe of wonder is what Gemini is after. To share that with other sparkling minds would be sublime.

To have the ability to be different than you were is a magic power. To rethink what you've taken for granted is a high art. Friendship is a flying carpet.

In third position, rounding off the first quarter of the zodiac, Gemini is still one of the youngest signs, with so much more ahead of it than behind.

Aries was searching for contact. Taurus was searching for meaning. Gemini is searching for freedom of movement, and it's not until the next stop down the line, in the realm of the crab, that the zodiac begins to grow up and approach the search for wisdom.

But even without the advanced consciousness that later signs aspire to, a myriad of blessings sprays out of the fountain of everyday existence when you approach it that way.

Regardless of how stuck human consciousness gets, bright possibilities arise at every intersection, where it's up to you, some fine spring morning, to invoke the power of the crossroads and choose how close or far away to stand from the splashing fountain.

It's your choice whether to close your eyes and bask in the refreshing currents, or dive into the foaming pool, or keep walking with a smile, knowing you're carrying vast possibilities, and that you, in fact, are a fountain.

GEMINI DRAGONHEAD/SAGITTARIUS DRAGONTAIL

From the big picture to the local view

With Sagittarius behind you and Gemini ahead, you're departing from the big picture and heading toward the local view. Often the reverse path is more appealing, because it's less messy. Like strong lysergic acid, your mind's so compelling it's easy to trip out and get lost there, so it's up to your friends and your body (and your friends' bodies) to reach in and pluck you out. You're journeying from exotic locales to the air you breathe and the ground you walk on, zooming in from generalities to specifics. After hobnobbing in past-life halls of power, you're after the extraordinariness of the ordinary, which admits you to a fantastic realm that may look normal but becomes a multidimensional playground when you get inside it. Because the number of things you want to do will always dwarf the amount you're getting done, it's all about opening your heart as much or more than your mind.

63

From
the local view to
the big picture

GEMINI DRAGONTAIL/SAGITTARIUS DRAGONHEAD

With Gemini behind you and Sagittarius ahead, you're departing from the local view and heading toward the big picture. That doesn't mean ignoring what's in your immediate vicinity, just not getting so wrapped up in the scenery that you lose track of the map. Throughout your reincarnational journey you shapeshifted through so many variations on the theme of being human that you don't need to keep adding more and more so much as fire up ideas big enough to stretch your imagination and do justice to the full scope of your ride. You'll never understand half of what the gods are telling you, but don't let the fact you're a cosmic fool keep you from galloping your centaur high into the eyries of dragons. Human foolery appears like emergency flares from that perch, because the more we stumble around down here, the more we draw the attention of celestial forces that need us to show them where to send their roadside assistance. Along with many other skills, you're a mouthpiece through which the gods sometimes speak, which doesn't mean you always have to know what you're doing, just that your willingness to serve goes a long way.

CHAPTER FOUR

Through the ages, some existential itch seems to keep humanity restless and searching, though we don't always know what for.

History's sages tell us that no amount of material prosperity will satisfy somebody impoverished within. Lacking a spiritual center, external gains only feed the hungry ghost in us who wants more and more.

It's equally true, however, that a person whose inner nature is prospering can't get far without external necessities of food, water, shelter and clothing.

So, while materiality without spirituality tends to inwardly impoverish a person, spirituality without grounding in the material plane detaches them from the earth. Somewhere between the two lies the happy medium the fourth sign is searching for.

After the wild and windy journey of the twins, Cancer is cautious of overexposure and seeks refuge by securing its place in the world. But if security is bought at the expense of inner truth, the belonging Cancer seeks carries a price too dear for this practical and thrifty sign.

The Buried Treasure of Cancer: The Art of a Perfect Fit

N OW THAT THE JOURNEY OF INDIVIDUATION HAS BEEN launched by Aries, deepened by Taurus, and blown open by Gemini, Cancer introduces the element of belonging.

Finding your place in life is the great modern conundrum, and it may be the main dilemma that distinguishes this age from earlier. As tough as life got then, people knew where they belonged. They weren't consumed by trying to figure out who they were and where they fit.

In today's world, most of us can only dream of such a fit. It's the rare person nowadays that truly knows who they are and what they're doing, and what they're doing contributes something meaningful to the world, which becomes a perfect fit.

Spiritual advice warns us not to get weighed down by material possessions, but I think humanity has more of the opposite problem—we haven't gotten weighed down enough, haven't sunk into the muck of incarnation, haven't faced our shadows, been forced to remember the love we're made of and gained the many treasures of the deep.

Cancer has its own unique gifts. Unlike most marine or terrestrial creatures, crabs don't belong to either land or sea, but both, and can miraculously breathe water *and* air, reflecting the propensity for this sign to be one of the most resourceful.

Cancer is also one of the dreamiest signs, wandering between tides and tide pools, sandy beaches and submerged caves, sifting memories and spotting movements that could be predators or prey.

Wanting to be useful, wishing to do its part, heeding the advice of others but also needing plenty of time to figure out things for itself, for a long while the practical and dreamy sides of this sign dwell in relatively peaceful coexistence.

But over the years, as adult responsibilities intrude more and more into its dream space, a crab must learn which childish notions to leave behind, and how to trade the transitory dreams of youth for those majestic dreams that fire its soul and carve its place in the world. For Cancer, growing up can be so poignant and fraught it never ends. This could be the one sign of the zodiac that never grows up because it's always growing up.

To find its fit, more than almost any other sign Cancer needs to be unrushed. You can't locate where you belong in today's complicated world till you unlocate all the places you *don't* belong, which you may have gotten lured into because they promised something that maybe didn't work out that way.

Most people scurry about day-to-day business, juggling responsibilities to make ends meet, rarely questioning their deeper purpose. For water- and air-breathing Cancer to excel at daily routine without uncovering its deeper purpose risks getting marooned in one of its environments at the expense of the other.

But to dive impetuously into a fantasy risks getting marooned in the opposite direction. So rather than marching straight ahead, Cancer moves sidewise, crabwalking, which buys time for its inner nature to grow into its outer existence. But such zigzagging can be hard for people to interpret, including Cancer itself, and make one dizzy.

Crabs have a knack for placing things off to the side, especially when they recognize that the significance of those things is going to take further growth for them to fathom. One of Cancer's greatest but least-known talents is being smart enough to know when it's not smart enough.

Hesitation is an experience every Cancer signed up to explore, and for this ponderous sign, there are many variations on hesitation, some fear-based and some based on prudence, though it can take a long time to tell the difference.

Just as the first sign Aries blazes the most straightforward path through the zodiac, the fourth sign has the most gradual and meandering approach, which makes sense when considered within the progression of the zodiac.

Now that we've made it one-third of the way around the wheel, some contemplation is in order, to check one's conscience, summon one's resources and gather one's tribes. This last is important because it's a safe bet wherever Cancer's going it's going to need kith and kin for support. Though some crabs tend to be hermits, most move in groups, yet they remain tentative, as if uncertain how long any group's going to last, or how long they want it to.

Regarding love, along with being one of the most thoughtful signs, Cancer is one of the most tactile, hyperaware of the way things feel, like skin on skin, fabric against skin, food against the tongue, or the feeling of an awkward situation or job well done.

Similar to a crab carefully crawling over items on the shore, Cancer usually needs to gain the *feel* of something before deciding what to do with it. Cancer undergoes many growing pains trying to feel into what it really feels about things, and whether an awkward fit means time to move on or life is starting to make sense on some new level Cancer hasn't quite pried out of the sand.

But even when you're crystal clear about where you're going, like a crab scuttling into the sea, elemental forces of wind, wave and weather have their own ideas.

Improvisational finesse, while not generally the first response of this sign (who likes planning ahead), can become an acquired skill that is one of its most valuable.

The zodiac's eternal student, therefore its eternal teacher, eager to learn and pass on those lessons to others, Cancer is hungry to understand not just what something is but how it fits with other important somethings.

The Cancer in us is the most reliable source for deciphering *The Earth-User's Guide to Practical Human Being,* which Cancer spends much of its life trying to find, till enough time goes by for it to realize it may first have to write it, which requires a concoction of instinct and memory.

In the game I play of determining Sun signs of fictional characters, the highly vulnerable, ridiculously gullible and enormously loveable Charlie Brown has got to be a Cancer.

Naively expecting life to make sense, many crabs get hoodwinked by repetitious snafus and human error. If everyone were as naively sincere in their need for approval as Charlie Brown, though, wouldn't the world be a lovely place?

The Cancerian author Hermann Hesse repeatedly dramatized the conflict between fitting into society and going one's own way, as seen in the opening paragraph of his third novel, *Gertrude:*

> When I take a long look at my life, as though from outside, it does not appear particularly happy. Yet I am even less justified in calling it unhappy, despite all its mistakes. After all, it is foolish to keep probing for happiness or unhappiness, for it seems to me it would be hard to exchange the unhappiest days of my life for all the happy ones. If what matters in a person's existence is to accept the inevitable consciously, to taste the good and bad to the full, and to make for oneself a more individual, unaccidental and inward destiny alongside one's external fate, then my life has been neither empty nor worthless. Even if, as it is decreed by the gods, fate has inexorably trod over my external existence as it does with everyone, my inner life has been of my own making. I deserve its sweetness and bitterness and accept full responsibility for it.

That final assertion—*my inner life has been of my own making. I deserve its sweetness and bitterness and accept full responsibility for it*—marks the moment Cancer (or anyone) claims psychic ownership of their life, which can be the most profound turning point. (Sometimes this needs to happen more than once.)

Though he wrote most of his fiction and essays in the early 20th century, the German-Swiss author's mystical coming-of-age tales anticipated (and helped bring about) the youth revolution that would explode a half century later in the 1960s.[3]

Like a Hesse protagonist, sooner or later many Cancers realize the ways of being that they inherited fail to serve. Picking up and leaving well-established grooves, though, rarely comes easy to a clawed animal; and hermit crabs, particularly, are mortally vulnerable after exiting their shell.

From the viewpoint of concerned parties attempting to coax it out, Cancerian resistance can try one's patience. After all, some crabs are distinguished in the animal world not just for having two ways to breathe, but for having a single colossal claw as well as nine more modest ones. This could indicate that although this sign is generally reasonable, if that giant claw seizes a way of being, heaven and earth may be easier to dislodge.

I get the feeling that while laboring to convince Cancers they've gotten stuck, although they usually listen, they're nodding at all the great advice you're laying on them while planning to go their own damn way as soon as your back is turned.

I've learned such obstinacy may come from innate knowing more than recalcitrance, though it's not easy to tell the difference, especially because Cancers tend to keep so much under their shell.

A close friend of mine has a Cancer son named Erick, who, between three and five years old kept trying to swim with the help of parents and friends, and finally at six began swimming lessons at the town pool. After each lesson ended, though, without his teacher to physically support him, Erick couldn't manage to stay afloat and push his light elfin body through the water.

The following summer our families were on vacation at the Rhode Island seashore, where one afternoon I looked down from the hotel balcony and was flabbergasted to spot Erick swimming briskly up and down the length of the large crowded outdoor pool, smoothly navigating floats

---

[3] *My Belief* and *Autobiographical Writings* are where you can find Hesse's marvelous essays, which I relish as much or more than his better-known novels.

and bodies with a huge smile, then turning around and doing it all over again.

Later when I asked what made him able to do that, he shrugged. Perhaps now that the quest which had taken half his young life had been consummated, and he'd proven his ability to himself, swimming already seemed so natural it was a done deal, and with modesty characteristic of his sign, Erick was uncomfortable with the attention I was lavishing on it.

It dawned on me that all along Erick might've been slowly and methodically internalizing the mechanics of propelling his body through water, without putting them all together until some somatic alchemy decided *now I will swim,* a rite of passage no outside pressure was able to accomplish. Once the transformation was complete, it seemed nothing could stop him, but until then it seemed nothing could *start* him.

It's hard to spot the missing link between not being able to do something for years and then flawlessly executing it, but I think this kind of situation arises when Cancer's conscious and subconscious minds unite.

One of the most valuable lessons this student of life can learn is timing, so that it neither pushes itself too soon nor lags behind, instead coordinating each important move with its season. The Ecclesiastical lyric to "Turn, Turn, Turn" would make an excellent chapter in *The Earth-User's Guide to Practical Human Being:* "A time to every purpose under heaven...."

The fourth sign may take long to come of age. It may be uninterested in the passing show that captivates others. Its ego may take a smaller bite out of life than modern egos are wont to, but Cancer may be no less capable due to these restraints and might even grow stronger because of them.

Such resistance to being pushed may help Cancer avoid the kind of traps dramatized by Hesse protagonists who sell their soul for social acceptance and end up with neither. In the long run, Cancer's refusal to go where it's not ready to may prove more wise than foolish—but there's always the danger of a Crab remaining so long in its shell it gets trapped.

Regardless of how seasoned and experienced Cancer gets, it's likely to remain hungry for understanding how things fit together, how *this* relates to *that,* and *that* relates to some other thing, like a genealogist sketching a family tree of metaphysical relations throughout the universe.

Many people born in this sign continue exercising their minds long after others let go of that need, which makes crabs excellent counselors, coaches, artists and therapists. And when a crab gains a certain maturity, its perceptions tend to get very rich, especially if it has resolved the main Cancerian quandaries of what to hold onto and let go of.

Remembrance falls squarely in the domain of Cancer, who has big-claw tenacity to hold onto things longer than other signs might. I think Cancerian memory resembles an underwater museum teeming with indispensable items organized in some eclectic way Cancer could never explain, but counts on.

The psychic side of this sign often has to do with everyday affairs more than exotic ones. In the 1990s my Cancerian girlfriend Carol told me that in her senior year of high school she got brochures from several colleges but knew she only needed to interview at one. When I asked how she knew which one, she shrugged and said, "I just knew."

Like good ol' Charlie Brown, shrugging may be more characteristic of this sign than any other (except Pisces, as we'll see at the end of the ride), because the utter ridiculousness of human nature (including their own) never fails to amaze them.

Many crabs write off their intuitive knowing as common sense, but the common sense of Cancer is one of the unsung powers of the zodiac, such a mundane magic it's easy to miss. But then mystical awareness seems to go hand in hand with a creature who has ten legs, breathes water and air, and walks sideways.

Just as it's easy for people to underestimate Cancers like Charlie Brown, it's easy for Cancers to underestimate themselves—and to assume that what seems obvious to them seems that way to others, which is often not the case.

Learning to question habitual assumptions is great training for this sign, whose thoughts need frequent reshuffling to keep from crystalizing into hardened shells. Whether Cancer locks into a path true to its soul or gets washed down a detour into some backwater, once it establishes pattern it's much easier to keep going that way than untrack and start over. So it behooves this sign to get off to a good start, a need that probably contributes to its hesitancy.

It's as natural for the student of the zodiac to want things to run smoothly and want everyone around them to get along as it is for a child, but at a certain point it becomes essential to ask, "Yes—but at what cost?"

Going along with the crowd is a survival tool in the animal world where a crab might end up in the gullet of a seagull. For a creature with succulent inner parts and little ability to gaze upward, it's not undue paranoia to imagine a sky full of winged predators.

Some crabs harness their fear into powerful initiations. One of my closest Cancer friends is an internationally renowned Grandmaster with black belts in many martial arts. With such accomplishments you might expect to bump into someone resembling The Mighty Thor, but if Richard were standing in line next to you at a supermarket you might think he was a Little League coach. His smallish size, relaxed demeanor and quickness to laugh betray few clues he's one of the world's most proficient warriors.

In exhibition, I watched him unarmed take out three young black belts who towered over him brandishing weapons, utilizing a series of moves he later broke down for us, which, without the antagonists present, seemed as effortless as washing dishes.

His specialty is simplifying each country's martial arts to the most essential moves that various cultures have in common. Cancer thrives on such essentialization, which goes a long way toward developing a perfect fit.

I believe most Cancers grow accustomed to withholding their power, which is why rigorous disciplines like martial arts, dancing, athletics, sailing, playing music, skiing, snowboarding, surfing, hiking, sexuality or making things with their hands can work wonders. (Those dexterous claws tend to make skilled potters, weavers, breadmakers, lovers, musicians and massage practitioners.)

It's natural for Cancer to attend to others simply because it feels good, and because this sign of creature comforts is quick to sense what others need to make them feel at home. (Remember that the crab carries its own home around with it.) Wanting folks to be comfortable seems a main common denominator of what I call the Hospitality Corner of the zodiac: Cancer, Leo and Virgo.

Regular rituals, especially including liquids, such as teatime (as in the U.K. where it's traditional to break for tea more than once daily), as well as tropical beaches, hot springs and steamy baths, appear to have an especially rejuvenating effect on this maritime sign. Perhaps the descent into healing currents reactivates in-utero memories that conjure a crab heaven of blissfully floating with every need met.

The perfect fit Cancer yearns for rarely arrives without extensive searching. Slow steady gains (punctuated by quantum leaps, like Erick's in the pool) constitute the main mode of the journey, because crabs tend to evolve gradually and are fairly incompetent at faking it. They're more likely to be raw and real than smooth and disingenuous. Even when Cancer manages to pull off a bit of ego bluster it's not usually long-lasting, because just underneath, like softshell crabs, their vital parts remain exposed. Which makes many people born in this sign quick to spot their own ridiculousness.

Intimate relationship with Cancers can be prickly because they require frequent solitude but also frequent engagement. They need protection—until they don't, then they need protection from protection! Their longing to be snugly enclosed, yet free to dream and wander, is something their partners will probably go through a few changes over.

If you get involved with a Cancer you should realize that though they may frequently vanish into sand holes, they rarely wish to abandon contact for long and need to know you'll be there when they come out.

A high-water mark in Cancer's relationship journey occurs when it knows itself well enough to identify when it needs detachment or engagement. If it learns to deliver that communiqué straightforward rather than sideways, Cancer clears a major hurdle.

When a crab figures out where it belongs and who it belongs with, it tends to sparkle with graciousness and insight. Its ability to care for others equips Cancer to be an attentive listener. Its rapture at what it means to come home after being long gone can make it a most accommodating lover or housemate to come home to. And when things get crazy, with one of the zodiac's most prominent senses of humor, a crab can shrug it off and focus on the more important stuff.

Many Cancers are well-suited for supporting roles that unexpectedly morph to leadership positions. Years of curiosity about what makes things tick often grant them more capacity to lead than they or others realize. Their instinctual wisdom may not make them the best *explainers,* but they excel at the kind of teaching that comes from modeling the most intelligent ways to operate, which others can follow by paying attention to little things Cancers do, even more than what they say.

In the Beatles, Ringo was the Cancer, thus could be easily taken for granted. For decades he seemed the weak link in the chain, the sad-sack misfit tucked in the shadows. But in recent years, as hot young drummers try to replicate his rock-steady rhythms and subtle changes of time, it has become evident it's hard to do what Ringo made look so easy. He was the all-powerful eye of the storm, whose staunch unflappability kept the band on track amidst a hurricane of fame and ego.

If you're fortunate enough to have a Cancer in your life, you can gain many gems if they trust you enough to open their treasure chest.

I see Cancer as the sign of writing, exemplified by Hermann Hesse, Ernest Hemingway, George Orwell, Helen Keller, as well as songwriters Greg Brown, whose tunes resemble three-minute novels, and the inimitable Cat Stevens, who almost singlehandedly (along with Donovan [a Taurus]) injected spiritual mysticism into AM radio.

Writing depends on imagination and memory, particularly what actors call sense-memory—the ability to dredge up physical sensations related to emotional events. Cancer's tendency to hold onto the past, while sometimes vexing in daily life, can excel in the imaginative arts.

The crab's tendency to keep far more under its shell than it lets out is illustrated by Hemingway's famous iceberg theory of writing: the idea that the most important part of a story is what's left out, and by eliminating everything inessential, the impact of the *story below the story* will strike readers more powerfully than anything stated, a wisdom I did my best to inject into this book by trimming my words and ideas more times than I could count.

Cancer is the great quest of learning where to belong, how to fit, who to trust, what to hold onto. These crabby affairs must be tended with diligent care because now that the zodiac has made it through its first third, it's crucial to hone navigational skills for the remaining two-thirds.

Unless this stage of the journey yields orientation and belonging, when things get complicated as the signs advance, the zodiacal ride may veer off the tracks, and way down at the far end, where the view looks much different than here, a soul can get flung apart.

Perseverance is the fourth sign's greatest asset, and no sign has more. When Cancer latches on to what it knows it wants and keeps going that way, it grasps the art of making every place home, because regardless of how long you're going to be there or what you're going to find, you may as well inhabit each living moment as if it were a perfect fit.

78

CANCER DRAGONHEAD/CAPRICORN DRAGONTAIL

From self-sufficiency to interdependence

With Capricorn behind you and Cancer ahead, you're departing from self-sufficiency and heading toward interdependence. The urge to do everything yourself may be noble, but you've come back to summon the circle—which means flipping your foibles into a communal way of operating rather than stuffing them under a crab shell. No shame in feeling overwhelmed, delegating power or asking for help. In past lives you were a dominant figure, set apart and above. You came back to get down into a life based on your kinship more than your glory. Vulnerability may be scary but beckons your dragon to find its place in the world, rather than forcing the world to make way for it. The problem with powerful people is they cast a lot of unconscious shadow. The belonging you crave won't arrive till you decide what not to belong to. You'll know you've come home to your tribe by the way it feels, and by how willing those around you are to meet your frailty as much as your strength.

From interdependence to self-sufficiency

CANCER DRAGONTAIL/CAPRICORN DRAGONHEAD

With Cancer behind you and Capricorn ahead, you're departing from interdependence and heading toward self-sufficiency. You're here to be a new kind of leader, who leads by inner truth more than ego and helps others find their own way. Wielding this kind of power is rare. Few role models exist because you're becoming your own. You can tell you're on track when your search for mastery raises everything in its way, which is why your journey is so prolonged and gritty. To climb that mountain you're grasping the reins in a chariot of paradox drawn by goats and dragons: The farther you climb, the more you realize how much farther there is to go. The more you awaken, the more you realize how unawake you are. Once you learn it's taking so long not because you're incapable or off-track, but because the route to authentic mastery has no shortcuts, the rest of the road opens. You know you're getting close when the world starts giving you what you want not because you're forcing it to but because you can't stop loving it

Astrology is the art of portraying human being. By dabbing some Taurus here, splashing some Gemini there, in the hands of an able practitioner the zodiac stretches, swirls and condenses into an impressionistic portrait. Out of the raw materials of the signs a figure emerges, which, as with all artistic renditions, is made of elements used countless times before, but in some new blend. If the portrait is rich and deep enough, astrology holds a mirror to the soul.

Where Cancer gives way to Leo, the early zodiac gives way to the midsection or core of the quest. Energies that have been used to establish the journey are now free to dig deeper into the process.

Like its namesake, Leo has a fierce appetite to sink its teeth into something juicy, which the zodiac hadn't gotten to previously but was on the way toward: self-actualization. Each of the first four signs, while presiding over their special interests, has also been blazing a trail to the land of the lion, where life becomes art.

Leo's Leap into Embodiment: The Art of Life Itself

Tucked beneath your personality, your soul crouches like a hungry lion, ready to pounce on superficiality and shred artificial existence. Leo is the summons to be so true to yourself you take the leap that turns living into an art.

Launching your life art won't banish your problems, but it will make you become less like everyone else and more like yourself.

Happiness doesn't come from eliminating problems but from eliminating the wrong problems (that diminish you) and bringing on the right ones (that summon your fuller presence and provoke your greatest growth).

Life art derives from the way you look at things, a perceptual filter that strengthens each time you use it. Becoming an artist isn't a complicated and baffling procedure reserved for a chosen few—you only have to see yourself as one. Once you do, you become one. The more you treat yourself like an artist, the more the world does too. The best part is no one's authorized to say otherwise. It's that simple, but it can take a whole life to master.

Art is the expedition to identify that which you love. We knew this once but forgot. In childhood, before you knew you were supposed to see things a certain way, you saw them *your* way. As you grew, your way of seeing things was influenced more and more by the way others saw them. The first time you saw a red mailbox, it may have been a portal to another dimension. Not so much the twentieth time, as it shrank to a metal box. When you claim the right to see things your own way, you can dive through mailboxes to Tanzanian skies.

Few things provide depth of meaning like art, because the best art, unlike the lion's share of academia and religion, captures profound insights beyond preachy didacticism. To do justice to those insights, time has to compost them down inside you, where they can undergo the alchemy enabling them to rise one day as original thoughts, something desperately needed during the intellectual wasteland of our age.

Leaping into life as an art often draws vivid responses from those around you, which bounce back from the force of your leap. Especially in the playground of intimate partnership, what bounces back at Leo the most is the news you can't get away from yourself no matter how hard you try.

So, since you can't get away from yourself you might as well fall in love with yourself. In the most non-egotistical, genuine, childlike, open-hearted way, you may as well fall head over heels in love with this perfectly imperfect human vehicle your soul chose to climb in and ride through the tangled underbrush of a single life like a Maserati.

Many people resist falling in love with themselves and associate those kinds of ideas with narcissism and egomania. If the idea of falling in love with yourself fails to grab you, you can fall in love with life, because since it's your life, it amounts to the same thing.

The Leo in you knows you can do anything truly in you to do. Knowing you can do anything that's yours to do is different from knowing you can do anything. A lion may be the most powerful lion in Africa but can't do what an elephant can. Nor should it. Once you get your inner lion on, life, like a poker game, is prone to declare *I see you and raise you.*

Leo is what happens when you meet everyday existence with soul. As your life surges with the spirit to express what it means to be you, it compels you to make creativity the main response you expect from yourself at every turn. If you choose to live that way, like many artists you may gain the sense that your creativity isn't really yours but comes from some mystic source you can channel and mold.

Leo rules physical activities that push your limits, and camaraderie of spirit that replaces society's costume ball with a striptease. Out go masks of appearance, in comes authenticity as the basis for connection, because it's much juicier to hook up soul to soul than ego to ego, and who wants to make love with their clothes on?

> *All the true vows*
> *are secret vows*
> *the ones we speak out loud*
> *are the ones we break.*
> *There is only one life*
> *you can call your own*
> *and a thousand others*
> *you can call by any name you want...*

From *All the True Vows* by David Whyte
© 1997, 2004 by David Whyte (courtesy of Many Rivers Press)

Whyte identifies true vows as silent rather than spoken, stripping the external component, eliminating the need to play to the crowd at the expense of inner truth, the Achilles Heel of this sign.

Silent vows go deep, because grasping your one true life demands fidelity between you and *you* more than between you and anyone else. You don't need consensus or approval. You need a heart-to-heart sit-down with yourself: 'Look, I've been watching you play the game, putting the big things off, delaying your arrival, holding back your love, living *as if* this life were your own. I have stunning news for you: *It is*!'

Leo feeds on honest self-confrontation, tantamount to entering a lion's den. Few Leos (or any other sign) linger there because it's messy and it's scary. Instead of departing the unexamined life, they curl up inside it and snooze.

Leo is the lion in you who longs to leap beyond equivocation and compromise into the life you were born for. That life races through your body like sacred fire, whose words are invisible until you die enough ego-deaths to read them.

Underneath your name, inside your personality, deeper than your body, a soul-spark flickers, yearning to ignite creative force packed in your core. If you gain a billion dollars and the admiration of millions but fail to ignite that spark, when you die it will be as if you'd done nothing. If you fail at everything else but ignite the spark, your soul will rest easy when your body dies.

When your body dies your soul will go on. While you're on this side of the great divide, your job is to blaze like a lion who throws back the darkness of the unlived life.

Self-actualization isn't about *How Great I Am!* so much as *me-as-vessel*. The more you embody the unique role your soul came here to play (and there's at least a lifetime's worth to learn about *that*), the stronger evolutionary forces you're able to channel. The stronger evolutionary forces you channel, the better the universe can play *its* role, because you're pulling off your part in the Karmic Theater, which allows the rest of creation to play its part with less resistance from you gumming up the works.

As your lion arrives, others will get drawn to the fire. Or repelled, but if your leap into embodiment pushes some people away, that may not be a bad thing. Like strong magnetism, the arrival of a big cat attracts and repels but rarely goes unnoticed.

Young children provide great examples of this, because until their authenticity gets drummed out of them, they have no choice but to be themselves, regardless of what others may think. Adults, not so much. Adulthood is the time we have to learn all over again many things we knew in childhood.

The groundbreaking Leo author Ray Bradbury wrote a provocative essay called *Who Owns What?* It is mostly a list of items, next to which he placed the name of whoever in writing, painting, sculpture or music he felt had poured the most soul into each. For example, sunflowers, which Bradbury asserted were owned by Vincent Van Gogh, because who else took sunflowers so deeply into their soul and hurled them onto the canvas with brush strokes so bold a blind man could read them?

Ownership of this kind can seem so material-oriented it'll rub spiritually minded people the wrong way. But in the spirituality I embrace, ascension is reserved for our journey out of the physical plane, while owning your life is the name of the game around here.

One of the strongest lessons I've learned is that failing to get what you love over and over is infinitely better than never failing because you never tried. I've failed to gain my heart's desire and fallen flat on my face more times than I care to mention, and can live with that much better than if I'd never dared myself to go after it.

When I was nine I saw a vision of my future as a book author in San Francisco. For about forty years I didn't know why San Francisco, because I grew up in Connecticut, where, like any budding writer, not only did I write up a storm but read voraciously. Mostly I read Ray Bradbury, whose prose I soaked into my pores. I probably learned as much from his stories as from the world around me, especially after one autumn afternoon in 4th grade when I crashed into the appalling realization that my parents weren't who they seemed to be.

What precipitated this collision was submitting an original poem for an elementary school assignment, where I got inside the mind of a spider, and having my teacher accuse me of plagiarism. She couldn't believe such words could've come from someone my age. But neither could she locate that poem in any of the books she hurriedly checked.

After school, my mother found me in bed crying, with the crumpled-up page in my hand, the teacher's red letters scrawled across it. When I uncrumpled it and showed it to her, though she didn't say so, I could tell she wasn't so sure I'd written it either. This was like getting kicked twice by a giraffe.

I took refuge in the passageway that linked one part of our three-story Colonial house to another, where I used to hide for hours, reading comics and cradling my cat.

Huddled in the dark, I reasoned that adults couldn't believe me because they'd strayed too far from their own childhood and were busy pretending to be something they're not. They couldn't recognize the magic that enabled me to get inside the mind of a spider because they'd abandoned their own magic.

They've forgotten, I told myself. *They're pretending to be something they're not. They've forgotten what this is like. They've lost their magic.*

How could this be?

How could they lose a magic I knew I was never going to lose?

Or—had they ever had it?

I thought about whether adults had magic when they were young, then lost it, or never had it in the first place, and I decided they must've had it—or else where did I get it from?

I sat chewing this over till I concluded that if the world commits some grand larceny between my age and theirs, stealing the most important thing of all from kids like me, I was gonna have to go through a helluva lot to keep my magic alive.

I vowed that whatever happened to them was *not* going to happen to me. No matter how old I got, I would never let anything steal my magic. *Never.*

Then I crawled out the far end of the tunnel into the unused portion of our attic, where I realized the best way to keep my magic alive was going to be by writing, and I made myself a little writer's studio up there, with desk, chair, dictionary, typewriter, paper and pencils.

Over the years I forgot about my vow. For three decades that day in the tunnel lay buried till a therapy session brought it out.

The therapist had me dialogue with my younger self, who told me not only had I kept my vow through the years, but I'd kept it so well I'd never even let him out of the tunnel until that moment, which released a flood of tears in me.

Although I blanked my vow after making it, I didn't blank my need to write, so I wrote through my teens and twenties but only got a handful of poems, stories and articles published here and there, while unpublished book manuscripts began to pile up.

By age thirty, in Berkeley, California, I'd grown bitter, and envious of writer friends who didn't seem much more talented than me but passed me by on the train to success, posting columns for *The New York Times* and piling up published manuscripts.

Gaining no foothold in the world of book publishers, I'd recently switched to the comic book industry. I wrote for years there, too, but only managed to get a few scripts sold, though I gained employment as editor and promotion director.

While wallowing in nonpublication blues, a guy I knew from comics, who'd heard of my lifelong infatuation with Bradbury, out of the clear blue phoned one evening to tell me if I could make it to Los Angeles the next day, I could meet Ray in his home and interview him.

That night I was unable to sleep. While the sun rose I took BART to Oakland, where I rode a bus to LA, got a ride to the famous writer's house, and in his living room, sitting cross-legged on his white shag carpet, we spoke of his stories (which I knew by heart) and of comics, writing and other passions. In the photos I'm incandescent from the proximity of my idol, who confided he could tell writers by a certain light in their eyes, which he said he saw in mine.

The lion in that 66-year-old Midwestern tale spinner was more virile than anyone I'd met. Ray was a tireless advocate for getting people to trust their muse. Lit from within, he ate up life like a kid in a candy shop. He poured his soul into everything he did, and never seemed to get over the fact he'd found a way to make a living planting dreams. His life force dwarfed mine but seemed made of childlike innocence. I learned that day the genuine royalty of our time may have fame and fortune, but what makes them royal is none of it goes to their head. Through all the hubbub and adulation their heart stays open.

In the following year, during an attack of especially low self-esteem, Ray told me, "Mark, there's nothing wrong with your writing. If you want to succeed, don't worry how much you're getting published.

"Don't obsess on books or magazines about writing. Don't worry about teachers, workshops or trainings. There's only one thing you need to do."

"What?"

"*Write.*

"Just write. Write every day, whether you want to or not. Write through rain, snow, sleet or shine.

"And don't talk about your writing till it's done, or you'll use up the juice you need to write. Save it. Let your pen do the talking. After you get it out you can talk about it all you want, but you may not want to because you'll want to get on with the next writing."

I wish I could say I followed my mentor's super-clear leonine advice, and I did, for a while, but not to the letter. Eventually I always got thrown off by my relationship dramas, money blues and lack of self-belief. As clear and strong as it was, I failed to take Ray's words to heart.

Flash-forward twenty years: In 2005, I got a manuscript accepted by North Atlantic Books, which, despite its name, was located in the San Francisco Bay. The publisher was nibbling on my hook, asking for rewrites. I'd only had a bite like this once, decades before, from Peregrine-Smith, but that was the one that got away, due to my twenty-something confusion, and I knew this was my big chance, especially because San Francisco was where I'd seen my future way back when.

The manuscript was the story of my apprenticeship to a wizard under the giant Redwoods of the Santa Cruz Mountains. Staring at the first page on my computer screen, I told myself, '*You're a writer.* You've known it since you were a kid. Your parents knew it. Your friends have always known. Ray knows it. This is your chance to prove it.'

I said aloud, "I don't know if I can turn this rough account of my sex-crazed misadventures in love and astrology into a bestseller, but if there's any way to do it, by the gods I *will*. I'm going to write seven days a week till I deliver the goods."

It worked.

Two years later, after exhaustive rewrites to balance the mystical and mundane sides of my tale, *2012: Crossing the Bridge to the Future* was published internationally, translated into different languages, and became a bestseller. Emails streamed in from readers around the world, with heartfelt outpourings of how much my story moved them. Reading those missives to my wife Marcella brought up very deep feelings in me, and made me weep.

Being escorted through the publishing house the first time I visited, where the staff huddled around to congratulate me like I was a rookie baseball player who'd won the Most Valuable Player for hitting it out of the park on my first season, a swell of pride rushed over me as it dawned on me that I'd kept my childhood vow. The only thing marring the event was my parents had passed on, so were not in San Francisco to celebrate.

Until you ride the lion, you may be in a decent marriage, bustling social life, well-paying job, but fail to ignite, like I might've if I hadn't taken Ray's advice.

Until someone lionizes, the world looks dimmer to them, because they're viewing a landscape that lacks their own illumination. Until you ignite, the universe is minus your light. Ironically, I've come to see holding back your radiance as selfish; it would be more selfless to let it out, give it all you've got, and take a bigger bite out of incarnation. It would be less selfish for you to illuminate others by shining on them.

The author meeting Ray Bradbury for the first time.

Leo is the sign of creativity, romance, embodiment, sign of the child, athlete, actor, artist, gymnast, yogini (I'm convinced people got yoga from cats). Leo is the irrepressible lion cub, the urge to come alive and play. It's the most contagious force around, because underneath the great modern shutdown, humanity's dying to break out of the zoo.

To live in the land of the lion you can follow the Law of the Pride, which states:

> You must do everything in your power to amplify the creative spark wherever you find it, and do nothing to extinguish that spark.

Down below who people think you are, below who *you* think you are, a core part of you knows exactly who you are and why you're here: to burst into bloom. To be yourself. To stick with your crazy truth until it gets somewhere. To follow the raw scent of the soul. Once you set that big cat in motion, it takes much more to stop it than keep going.

Some spiritually minded folks seem confused about selfhood. Self-actualization doesn't give you the right to lord over anyone. It's not about how great you are but how much life force you channel. It's an act of embodiment that turns the world into a place so worth showing up for, you can't bear to miss a moment.

Even though I forgot about my childhood vow, it didn't forget about me. It kept smoldering through the intercession of a handful of perceptive individuals I bumped into over the years. The first was a substitute teacher who took over 12th-grade English class one week in June. On his last day he drew me aside and said, "Mark, you have a unique and fertile imagination and rare ability to follow your muse, regardless of what everyone else is doing. I've seen this in a few other kids, who later lost it. The world took it away. I'd hate to see that happen to you."

"It won't," I assured him.

With a dubiousness that was probably just what I needed before high school graduation turned me loose on the world, he retorted, "That's what *they* said."

Just because someone is living doesn't make them *alive*. Just because they have eyes doesn't mean they *see*. Leo is the summons to fire up the radiant one within you, so you can navigate by central illumination rather than peripheral vision.

Many people live as if life's what they have to get through till something better comes along. While growing up, somebody taught them to dim their light. When making love, someone told you you were wrong. The mask you put on drew positive strokes from other masks, growing tighter on the skull till you forgot you were wearing it.

Each time a lion escapes the zoo, it inspires others to do the same, as we saw in the 1960s. The majority of baby boomers, born from the mid-1940s to the late '50s, have the deepest planet, Pluto, in Leo, because Pluto takes a long time to transit the twelve signs. Therefore millions of people have it in the same sign.[4]

Author Tom Wolfe, though I doubt he knew its astrological correlation, dubbed this group the *Me Generation,* referring to our self-fixation. Even though the moniker was seen as a slur more than compliment, the Pluto-in-Leo generation produced a worldwide roar. We needed that roar to banish Establishment conformity and break out of the System, because the System was defunct, and its psychic herd dogs were caging our spirits.

Our generational imperative to bust out catalyzed a revolution in consciousness that you can hear in the music of those years and the music it's still inspiring.

One of the most reluctant lions of the revolution was Jerry Garcia. Few people epitomize the positive and negative qualities of his sign better than the central driving force of the Grateful Dead.

---

[4] If you're a Leo, that means the Sun was appearing to pass through Leo during your birth, but you have many other planets, each passing through their own sign. Most of my close peers, regardless of their Sun sign, have Pluto in Leo.

Magnanimous, self-deprecating, brilliant, the lion inside the man remained fiercely uncompromising in artistic pursuits, but the man inside the lion sank into hard drugs that eventually took his life.

Unlike most modern media darlings, Garcia didn't seek fame, and fought against it. When commercial success finally arrived for the Dead, the increasing demands of it, similar to how they did for the Beatles, gradually became a prison for this boundlessly innovative songwriter and guitarist. To placate the masses who closed in on him like hyenas closing on a wounded lion, he kept cranking the machine.

Jerry's light still illuminates millions. His bottomless creativity and warm generosity run true to Leo. But the killing pressure to play to the crowd instead of breaking away to follow his truth was something he never got free of. What he ended up giving the world seems purer and healthier than what he gave himself.

The paradox of self-actualization demands that you believe in yourself while not getting hung up on yourself. Garcia never got hung up on himself, and that might have been part of the problem. I don't think he ever saw the brilliance of his own light.

The art of selfhood gets a bad rap in spiritual circles where people like to talk about the splendiferous day humanity will transcend ego. But such transcendence is often premature, because until a person claims their one true life, they're trying to transcend something they never fully embodied, trying to give away something that was never theirs.

The universe had good reasons for giving you the life you're currently wearing. It's no accident you are who you are and not someone else. When you grant yourself the benefit of the doubt that your soul knew precisely what it was doing when it chose the strange brew of absurd realities and unique talents that is you, you turn life into art. When you embody that life art, you lean on creativity as devotionally as some people lean on religion.

Self-actualization is not the final stage of the twelve-part journey, which still has more than halfway to go. But this step is crucial, because a good strong selfhood is needed, not as an ego feeder but as a sufficiently sturdy instrument to channel the greater cosmic forces that will begin streaming into the zodiac a few stages down the line.

From collectivity to individuality

LEO DRAGONHEAD/AQUARIUS DRAGONTAIL

With Aquarius behind you and Leo ahead, you're departing from collectivity and heading toward individuality. You gained past-life experience learning to think the way others thought, which postponed the full release of creative forces packed in you. Having been insufficiently tapped through the ages, that spiritual bank account accrued interest. As soon as you're ready, you can draw from vast funds, but the kicker is you have to know you're ready rather than just be kind of ready. You've got to get out of your own way. Your dragon is sitting on heaping mounds of creativity that await your willingness to be the absurdly flawed individual you are. Trust what you love and can't live without and let the rest go. Some throwaway ideas you let slip by might yield a whole life. The lion of your soul knows what it's after, but it's taking a while for the rest of you to catch on.

From individuality to collectivity

LEO DRAGONTAIL/AQUARIUS DRAGONHEAD

With Leo behind you and Aquarius ahead, you're departing from individuality and heading toward collectivity. Your past lives featured the blessing and curse of big selfhood, which granted you strength of character but resistance to merging. That strength can thicken to a skin of ego that prevents love from getting in and soul from getting out. You got fed up with counting on anyone who wasn't you, and that's a tough habit to break. The good news is allies are everywhere because even if you feel squashed down on the planet, your Aquarian Dragonhead grazes the ceiling of the universe. Most people speak Earth talk; you've come to decode the cosmos. The awakening of our time needs spiritual outlaws to subvert the dominant paradigm, overthrow the Rule of Ego and bring on the Rule of Love. The more you refuse to get drafted into the Polarity Wars, the more you help bring about *The End of Everything That Never Worked Right in the First Place,* by building a bridge from this strange modern disconnect to the unified field beyond, where dragons romp.

CHAPTER SIX

The human mind is a churning, whooshing, double-edged scythe that cuts ties binding us to ignorance, but when caught in delusion, it slices truth to folly while swearing otherwise. Those slices fall to the ground like seeds that grow further folly, trapping the bright human spirit in a husk of ignorance.

How a species could be capable of health and wholeness yet keep reaping the same toxic harvest we've been warned against time after time through history is not just a Virgo hell—it's everybody's. It weighs on Virgo more, though, because Virgo holds the moral imperative of the species, the part of us that knows you reap what you sow. At this halfway point of the twelve-stage journey, it's time for the zodiac to grow a conscience.

As the creation myth of virgin Persephone indicates, Virgo is the mediator between the heaven humanity could choose and the hell it keeps choosing, however inadvertently.

Persephone is a tale with several variations that was already old by the time the Greeks cobbled together their versions from earlier strands of myth. The story illustrates sexual desire, transgression of boundaries and the cyclical nature of seasons in which things die but sometimes return.

Most versions begin with young Kore (The Maiden) telling her mother Demeter (Mother Earth) she feels confined and restless within the boundaries Demeter has set, and longs to go out roaming. Like her distant father Zeus, who's up on Mount Olympus (and was never very good at honoring boundaries), she's antsy to bust out.

Demeter replies that for a comely, untested young goddess, the world is full of dangers, but as long as she's willing to remain in sight of the handmaidens she's going to send to keep an eye on the girl, she'll grant her request. Kore agrees, and along with her chaperones, sets off.

From the edge of a field, the ecstatic young woman spies a pure white narcissus growing on the other side of a stream. Though it will mean temporarily straying out of sight of the handmaidens, Kore crosses the stream and plucks the flower.[5]

Unbeknownst to her protectors, a fissure opens the ground and, as if he'd been waiting for her, up rushes the chariot of Hades, who grabs the girl, drags her down and, as the fissure snaps shut, steals her away to the underworld.

Tales differ regarding the specifics of how voluntary or involuntary is Kore's coupling with Hades down under. Whichever way that unfolds, she soon finds herself Queen of Hell, which renames her Persephone (Bringer of Chaos).

Persephone's new status is a mixed blessing. As an untested goddess, suddenly becoming second-in-command of Hell floods her with awesome new powers over life and death. However, though she's become co-ruler, she finds she can't get out of Hades, even for a moment, and soon longs for fresh air and wide-open spaces, similar to how she longed to depart her mother's confinement above.

Most versions of the story agree that however the dark god treats her during her abduction, once she ascends the throne, he treats her like an equal.

---

[5] Tales vary on which flower she picks, and I like the narcissus, which symbolizes self-knowledge.

Some versions suggest he has to because, with Zeus for a father and Demeter for a mother, Persephone has become every bit as powerful as he and, as the bringer of chaos, may be even more feared by gods and mortals than he is.

The handmaidens search far and wide but return to Demeter and tell her they can find no trace of the girl. For failing to protect her daughter, the wrathful goddess transforms them to Sirens, with the heads of beautiful women attached to the bodies of ravenous human-eating birds. Then the earth goddess sinks into a funk, which withers the mortal lands.[6]

Death spreads in the wake of Mother Earth's passing as she mournfully searches the world for her missing child, until she crosses paths with wandering deities who suggest her daughter may be in the underworld, because Zeus, knowing his brother had the hots for the girl, had given Hades permission to take her, and the dark king had been waiting for his chance.

Cold rage at her ex is now added to Demeter's anguish, bringing further ruin to mortal lands, until a crop blight threatens Zeus's master creation: the human race. To appease her and save them, Zeus sends clever Hermes, the only Olympian with carte-blanche to all realms, to figure out what the hell's going on.

When he arrives down there Persephone asks Hermes to take her back to the lands of the living, and he agrees, so long as she hasn't eaten any fruits of the underworld.

---

[6] The Sirens later famously make an appearance in *The Odyssey* when Odysseus has his crew tie him to the mast so he can hear their seductive song without diving to his doom like so many sailors.

However, she'd eaten half of a pomegranate's seeds, so Zeus decrees she must spend half of each year reigning alongside Hades (when Earth mourns and we have winter) and half in the sunlit lands (when Demeter is happy and we have summer).

As the agricultural sign, Virgo is born knowing death isn't The End but part of a turning wheel. Just as plants rise from the soil, bloom and die, and their fruit drops to the ground, seeding new life that rises, blooms and dies, the maiden's seedlike nature—her Kore-self—one way or other had to die so her fuller nature could be born.

Lacking the flower of self-knowledge is a naive state that pertains not only to the untested gullibility of youth, but the hazardous pre-awake state of humanity at large: the only species on Earth who hasn't grown up. Like a sleeping beauty, humanity slumbers through the ages without awakening its greater consciousness.

Like the story of the human race, a sense of inevitability haunts this tale from its beginning. As her father's daughter, the lusty young girl is bound to rail against limits: If we remain penned in the enclosures of those who came before us, we'll never learn who we are as independent beings.

But plucking the flower produces a whole other set of dangers, because self-knowledge brings more awareness of the darkness as well as the light. Once you go in and out of hell, you're not likely to forget what you saw there.

Between treacherous shadows and blinding light, our species stumbles down the road on its long slow climb toward higher ground.

The Mad Passion of Virgo: The Art of Changing What Is into What Ought To Be

IT'S THE MIXED BLESSING OF THE SIXTH SIGN TO CARRY PRE-scient awareness of how things *ought to be* alongside gritty awareness of the way things *are,* which divides the Virgo movie screen evenly down the middle.

On one side, crying needs and disjointed fragments fly by in stark contrast to the other side, which streams harmonious images of functionality and wholeness.

Such split consciousness drives Virgo nuts; any time this sign lavishes attention on the one creates an irresistible pull from the other, and the big question is if they will ever meet.

Between the sobering reckoning with what *is* and the relentless pull of what *could* be, humanity gets wrenched back and forth like Persephone. Such trial of extremes produces the mad passion of Virgo, who longs for the light, has wedded the darkness and must find a way through both.

The extent of what this sign is trying to accomplish out in the world varies considerably from Virgo to Virgo, but regardless of whether they have modest aims or grand ambitions, Virgo is the great plow horse of the zodiac, working the ground between the real and the ideal. Because the view appears strikingly different from each side, the Virgo experience often depends more on where Virgo's looking *from* than what it's looking *at*.

From the reality side, things look bleak: a late freeze threatens the planting, dry spells wither the soil, a plague of weevils demands constant vigilance to secure the harvest.

From the ideal side, miracles abound and crops flourish within the natural order of things without needing much help. Which view is truer? Or are they equally true? Might there be a third view?

Due to its strong need to step back and get a clear picture, perspective, as with a visual artist, means almost everything for this sign. To gain the right perspective, which places things in proper proportion to other things, Virgo has to try on many views, changing its vantage point, reviewing its data, renewing its vision. Amidst the change-ups, the divine satisfaction of a job well done is all most Virgos are after, but usually find in short supply.

The face of a Virgo is frequently impassive, revealing little of what's going on below, but when struck by a new way to look at things can burst into sudden radiance, like the late-summer sun breaking out from behind a cloud. Few things delight a harvest child as much as finding the unusual in the midst of the usual, and turning commonly accepted ideas on their heads.

Their restless conscience and hardy capacity make Virgos the type of people others confide in. People born in this sign usually make better listeners than talkers, and they are often reluctant to say anything unless they have something worth saying.

Human communications can mystify this sign, because Virgos take things so earnestly, they expect others to say what they mean and mean what they say. Hence they can puzzle over why human interactions get so wonky. Heart-to-heart talks can be manna from heaven for this sign, and the silent communion of souls who understand each other beyond the need for words even better.

Virgo is second to none at honoring the fine attributes and noble deeds of others and can be generous to a fault—but don't abuse that, because if this sign feels taken advantage of, it can bolt with no warning.

Virgo's need to weed out the inessential often causes it to question the ethics and efficacy of what it's doing and what's being done by others around it. Eventually many Virgos come to require honesty as the main prerequisite for friends and lovers, as any who transgress that boundary will soon find out. But Virgos first have to get honest enough with themselves to determine what they need, what they cherish, what they'll settle for and what they can't, which is more of a lifelong rite of passage than something they go through once when young.

It's not hard to befriend this sign, but rarer to have them fully let you in, a privilege they seem to reserve for a lucky few. Others who approach may sense a remote interior they can't quite reach.

A detached quality often makes Virgo seem incomplete, as though awaiting some final ingredient they may not know the identity of.

As hands-on as this earthy sign likes to get, one of the most important lessons Virgo learns is that how you see something makes all the difference as to what you can do with it. Like a farmer sharpening tools on the way to the field, Virgo needs to regularly clean used thought forms and replace worn-out paradigms.

Similar to Persephone, Virgo is searching for sacred ground, safe space and a sovereign realm to call its own. It's seeking forces to assist a healthy harvest.

Its skill of dividing the vital from the expendable prompts others to turn to Virgo when they need something sorted. The universe, too, tends to call on Virgo as Gaia's child, as if trees and plants lean in toward the young goddess's foray into the Great Wide Open.

Between constant pressure from the ultra-real side of the field and smooth sailing on the ultra-ideal side, Virgo plows back and forth. No sign is more conscientious, and none more haunted. None is more blessed, cursed, gifted and confused.

Though they frequently lapse into hazy mental states, Virgos can harness a clarity of thought so sharp it becomes fierce in its willingness to attack a puzzle the way a squirrel attacks a nut.

To do justice to this sign, who, out of the entire zodiac through the ages I believe has been the least accurately portrayed (for reasons that will soon become clear), I'm going to highlight the female version. I apologize in advance to the rest of my readers and invite you to do what women have been doing for centuries—extrapolate your gender variation from the dominant narrative.

Virgo is the great realist of the zodiac.

Virgo is the great idealist.

When Virgo is *on,* she's incredibly on. But being on demands not only diligent effort, it requires a downpouring of grace, which Virgo can't count on by snapping her fingers, therefore needs a threshing gang to help with the harvest, a coterie of comrades as wild and willing as she can be.

When Virgo is *off,* she tends to become ghostlike (as you might expect from the queen of the dead), as though life passes through her and she passes through life without much intercourse.

But that same objective neutrality can yield harvest vision that beams a grow light nurturing the hidden potential of others. Such vision enables Virgo to bring out the best in people, though the favor doesn't always get returned. It's easier for her to see than to be seen, which means souls who signed up for sixth position will be rigorously tested to find out who they can be for others before learning who they can be for themselves.

The previous sign having gobbled the lion's share of selfhood, Virgos tend to shy away from singing their own praises and offer contributions more for the sake of what they can accomplish than for glorifying the contributor.

In the parceling out of zodiacal ambition, it was Virgo's lot to be more concerned with effectivity than self-aggrandizement. Recognition and praise often bounce off a virgin like repelled suitors rather than get taken in and made love to. But too much non-recognition may cause Virgo to decline to recognize herself, and fail to sort her strengths from her weaknesses.

Virgo's greatest kinship is often with the nonhuman members of the threshing crew, because Mother Earth's child tends to experience herself as separate from most people. Many Virgos have to tap nature first to find their connection to humans, as if trusting the universal intelligence that runs through the garden of life comes easier than trusting fellow humans.

Here at the halfway point of the zodiac, we've arrived at the Get-Real sign, and getting real for Virgo is often a Hydra-like affair where resolving any problem yields three more. Despite conscientious effort, detail upon detail and need upon need pile up in the field till there's little room left to plow.

As the Get-Real sign, Virgos can't stop questioning why their efforts take so long to bear fruit: Is it because of flaws in their methods? Complications in their environment? Must they reinvent the wheel at every turn? Are they missing some key piece or subtle thread that makes all the difference? Are they too stubborn for their own good? Should they throw their hands up and walk away? Have they not yet gone mad enough to deal with a world gone even madder?

Being a very visionary sign but also a very realistic one, Virgo dreams of a streamlined approach that yields consistent results and may plow in that direction for a long time before getting there. Sometimes they arrive upon richly earned contentment, but soon as their back is turned, mischievous imps poke their pointed noses out of the tall grass to mess with the harvest.

As daughter of an earth goddess, the Virgo body is endowed with marvelous powers of sex and healing, which is a great boon, because a Virgo mind, sharp as it is, ranges from crystal clear to muddy sludge, and needs a body it can count on to take up the slack.

To coin an adjective, the body of Virgo is *polygraphic* and can function as a lie detector, indicating what they should and shouldn't eat, who they should get close to and shouldn't, and especially who to get sexual with and who absolutely not. However, such messages from the body may take a while to get through to the brain.

When the child of Mother Nature strays from her true nature, her physiology tends to act out with symptoms (often digestive). Virgos might be soaring along until bumping into a certain person, then feel hazy. Or dance with someone they never thought much of and find themselves on top of the world.

A Virgo whose body and mind align is something glorious to behold and just about all this sign is seeking, though it's anybody's guess when they'll get there.

Like young Persephone, after dwelling in the shadow of her harsh deity mother and presiding over the tormented pits of her dark lover, sooner or later Virgo must step out of the lands of others to claim her own sovereign lands. That passage usually occurs gradually, like slow-moving earth, rather than in one definitive moment, though such moments can accelerate the process.

Which means pushing against definitions and boundaries to find what she's made of. It means flirting with the dark side (something few Virgos can resist) in order to learn the nature of the light. It means breaking away from everyone else's catastrophes to claim the full erotic power of her own sovereign being.

Mediation is a skill Virgos are born with and can strengthen by learning to mediate between the extraordinarily functional parts of themselves and ridiculously dysfunctional parts. Like Kore they sometimes get thrown into hellish situations that force them to gain more power than they ever would've if they'd stayed out.

Even when young, some Virgos generate the aura of village elders, whom you don't want to unnecessarily bother. They can untangle knots with straight talk and lucid vision, though it's harder for them to apply such medicine to their own dilemmas.

Learning to discern what is and isn't yours, what's essential or optional, and what must be held onto or released are Virgo functions that replicate the role of digestive organs in the body, ruled by this sign, that choose which nutrients to retain and which to expel.

For Virgo, discerning occurs almost as often as breathing; they're the natural editors of the zodiac, trimming, pruning, tossing excess onto the burn pile, but often taking a long time to prosper.

An indication of whether Virgo is on track has to do with her capacity to give. It's not natural for Mother Earth's child to go long periods without giving. If she does, it indicates something's off. It can be hard for her mind to grasp the fix, though her body usually knows and sends clues in the form of aches, longings and ecstasies.

Virgo listens to many but trusts few, which means cultivating healthy harvests is more trial-and-error than sure bet. Only after clarifying what *isn't* are they likely to find what is. Only by wrestling with inefficiency can they become efficient. Only after many escapades avoiding its greater truth can this hard-working yet hard-partying sign land squarely on it.

Planted in the midsection, or belly, of the zodiac, the sixth sign has a lot to digest and features the zodiac's rarest blend of *willing-to-go-with-just-about-anything* and *impossible-to-please.* For the sign of discernment, it can be surprising how much they throw caution to the winds, but that's often how they release pressure.

Sandwiched on the left by rams, bulls, twins, crabs and lions, and by even more critters on the right, no other sign is this surrounded, has this much closing in on it, is so pressurized, yet capable of so much super-charged release.

As Virgo awakens to deep truths of body and soul, it enters a sweeping expanse of astronomic proportions, because, despite its down-to-earth reputation, Virgo is the most galactic sign, made of stars and planets galore.

The second-largest of all constellations in the sky, Virgo is the largest zodiacal constellation and farthest from Earth. Her luscious body beckons from the southern horizon in a starry pictograph that stretches bigger than the Big Dipper, so unfathomably distant that what appear to be the stars of her outline are actually galaxies, so far away they look like stars. If the reality-check of billions upon billions of stars appearing as a single star is hard to digest, you're beginning to glimpse the kind of forces this sign is reckoning with.

Knowing it's made of galaxies can recast the proportions of what Virgo is up against compared to what she's made of. And Virgo's always up against *something,* so that periods when she's only trying to strip the husk off two or three dilemmas can seem like glorious vacations.

It can be the most potent medicine for Virgo to consider she's vast enough to contain not just stars, but *worlds within worlds*. Like a desirous young goddess suddenly flooded with power, the galactic perspective can change everything.

If you harbor near-infinities, choosing which way to go at any given point must become based on something other than personal capacity— because Virgo's capacity is beyond measure. For a modest sign this can take a lot of head-scratching, because if you have multitudes within you, how in heaven or hell are you ever going to determine what to do with that?

Located next to the lion's den, Virgo generally frowns on drawing attention or outshining others and becomes acclimated to holding back. However, craving intercourse of the soul more than flirtations of the body, her reluctance doesn't indicate a lack but a plenitude of forces that demands a new narcissus: a wholly different scale of self-understanding, which honors the vast cosmic reach of her spirit without denying any of the rigors of her mortal form.

Of all the signs, I believe Virgo runs on *Sacred Invite*. With galaxies of unborn potential spinning within her, she rarely knows what to do with her huge erotic force until the universe summons her.

Like Penelope turning away suitors in *The Odyssey* while her husband's lost at sea, many Virgos spend their lives waiting for the invitation they can't refuse. More than any other member of the zodiac, this one craves the full release that only right livelihood can supply.

Until that invitation comes along, Virgo may get a myriad of things done but feel unsatisfied, knowing she hasn't done what she came for. Whether Virgo turns the waiting period into reverent vigil or quarrel with existence makes all the difference. This sign's operating instructions could be: Whatever you can't analyze you may as well dance with, and whatever you *can* analyze you may as well dance with even more.

Throughout the dance she's searching for something to serve that serves her as well. Most Virgos, for a long time, are much better at telling you what that *isn't* than what it is. Searching for sacred invite, the sign built to serve must spend countless hours learning what not to serve.

In our age service is often looked down upon, but in some cultures, and at earlier times, it was a sacred art, and those trained to practice it, like the Vestal Virgins of ancient Rome, were held in high esteem.

Virgo means virgin, and historic appropriation of that word has prevented the true nature of the sign from being recognized by astrologers, who often stereotype it as the prissy librarian or anal-retentive old maid who crosses her t's and dots her i's, while getting all her ducks in a row. Prior to Christianity, though, the word had a much different meaning. Rather than a girl who hadn't had intercourse, 'virgin' meant 'a woman unto herself.'

In ancient times, temple dancers were called virgins, fulfilling a function that in today's parlance has been called 'sacred prostitute.' If that seems an oxymoron, consider how Christian dogma split the divine and carnal sides of the feminine into the two Marys: the immaculate Mary, Mother of God, who gave birth without being penetrated, and the profane Mary, who never stopped being penetrated—Mary Magdalene, who ran around with the other Mary's son. According to this dogma, if you're born in a female body, you're a slut or a saint. If the notion of sexuality uniting you with God seems blasphemous, it may be because the split persists.[7]

In some matriarchal cultures it was believed that man couldn't get to the goddess without going through the priestess who was her divine avatar. He couldn't access the life-giving succor of the divine feminine without making love to its representative on Earth. Man needed the grace of the goddess to bless his journey and watch over his long nights. Certain women were trained to erotically dance in temple courtyards, enticing worshipers to make love with them. The priestess's body was understood to be a living temple within the larger temple, to seduce men into the kind of religion that could knock sense into their heads.

A virgin could make love with as many lovers as she chose, but she was a virgin because, as a woman unto herself, no man could own her. No one could use her for anything but the purpose she'd been trained for: bringing Heaven to Earth through the sacred mediation of her body.

---

[7] For more on the sacred prostitute, see the book of that name by Nancy Qualls.

Temple dancers were revered rather than reviled like modern prostitutes often are. Back then, the holy and the erotic weren't diametrically opposed. No one had to put them together because until Christianity came along, no one thought of splitting them apart.

The holy-lust version of female sex and power became anathema to early Church fathers. Demonizing the wild, primal, liberating eros of the unchecked feminine, they bound it in a psychic straitjacket that persists today between many women and their orgasm, many females and their power. The jacket doesn't only bind ecstasy but traps the life force, because sex isn't only pleasure-giving but life-giving, life-sustaining and life-renewing.

The moment power-mongers inserted God-the-Father between a woman and her bliss, the stage was set for historic misery, because men lost the key to the interior sanctuary of women, and women lost the primal wholeness they're still trying to reclaim.

The split lives on in modern culture: The name for the female crotch, *pudendum,* is Latin for 'mound of shame.' Hysterectomies derived from the notion that a woman who gets hysterical has too much uterus and should have it removed. Still today in some parts of the world that surgery, as well as clitorectomies—an abomination—are performed for dubious reasons.

Because of religious appropriation, I believe through the ages this sign suffered more misunderstanding than any, and must be radically reconstructed. As the sign most wedded to devotion, any true understanding of it requires banishing the catechism from the temple.

Like a temple dancer, a Virgo of any gender was born to serve. Once they figure out how *not* to serve and what *not* to serve, and find a way to serve that serves themselves, service becomes more akin to dancing than drudgery.

Orgasm too is a kind of service, because it burns out the gunk that collects from being incarnate in a body during a confused and toxic time on planet Earth. Modern civilization might be batshit crazy, but orgasm is one of the least mixed-up things on the planet.

Some Virgos and people with strong Virgo in their chart are drawn toward sex as healing. Apart from its ability to satiate desire, sexuality can loosen up trauma stored in the body. Longstanding wounds, inflamed by desire, rise toward the contact point of a lover's touch, where they can be released by orgasm.

True to her temple-dancing forebears, withholding such healing power can feel wrong to Virgo, as if she's breaking an ancient contract— which can be confusing if her body wants to make love to someone her mind doesn't, or vice versa.

Sacred sexuality often gets lost in a culture where sex is used to sell toothpaste. One reason modern culture is ignorant of the true nature and broad spectrum of sexuality is because, unlike earlier cultures, sexual wisdom is rarely passed from elder to younger. Rather, it's locked in the infamous black box that adults tell kids not to open.

The primary indicators of sexual distortion in mass consciousness are TV and movies, where breathlessness is either equated with one-night stands or forbidden fruit, occurring clandestinely, extra-maritally or if one of the lovers is about to die. Such melodrama exacerbates the historic split, as if getting turned on is a sin, and any couple who remains in a monogamous relationship for forty years has no chance of fucking each other's brains out.

In ancient China, widows whose husbands were slain in battle initiated young men into sex, serving two needs at once. On their wedding eves, Chinese daughters received pillow books from their mothers, illustrating positions they could try with their husbands. Sexuality wasn't demonized but illuminated.

Virgo is the desire to craft a healthy, sensual and abundant life. Figuring out how to do that can take a little bit of heaven and a lot of hell. The great Virgo irony is that the sign most qualified to make the world sane is the one most driven insane by it. Only someone with equal awareness of *what is* and *what ought to be* is likely to be as blissed out as they are tormented.

When Kore descended to the underworld and coupled with Hades, she became a divine instrument injecting her innocent purity into the troubled soul of mankind. Each time she leaves her fearsome mate to return aboveground, she gives the masculine alone-time to integrate all she'd brought to it. While she's away she gets to contemplate all she absorbed in her plunge, and reenter a virginal state where she can commune with nature, with the feminine, and with the depths of her own nature.

Every Virgo needs plenty of time alone and tends to get overwrought without it. More than complicated solutions to the perplexities that baffle this sign, Virgo often needs room to breathe, after which things may look much different. Alone time restores the sacred space this sign needs to purge invasive energies that block access to sacred invites. Sacred time can restore sacred rhythm, and the rhythm of the breath dances its own dance within us that we return to when releasing ourselves from outer rhythms.

When a Virgo claims its service and glory, it begins to preside over a third realm that's neither the realm of Demeter nor Hades, but its own sovereign lands, where its own life rhythms can transcend the herky-jerky rhythms of modern people at odds with themselves, and dance the great dance between spirit and matter.

Until she presides over her own lands, Virgo may know that existence should be more heavenly than hellish, but must go through several awakenings to discover what to do with that knowing.

It can take many lovemaking sessions to figure out how to make love. It requires repeated striving against your own blindness to cure someone else's lack of sight. It demands great dancing with the darkness to learn to live in the light.

If Virgo carries its need to serve too rigidly, it can get trapped in incessant doing, and the celestial harvest pouring out of the goddess's cornucopia spills on parched soil.

But if Virgo fails to rise up and fulfill some higher purpose, it can sink into torpor, knowing it's not being used for the reasons it should be.

Somewhere between trying too hard and giving up, Virgo may find peace at the end of the day, like sitting atop a grassy hill during a fine breeze and wrapping the stars around her like a blanket.

Virgo is the *feng shui* of life, a golden compass to redirect creative energies of the universe into more elegant flow. It's the tuner musicians use to adjust the pitch of their instruments, and the focusing dial on the TV of life (from back when TVs had dials).

When Virgo is in tune, it sets the tone for everyone. If you need something figured out, call a Virgo, unless what you need figured out is the Virgo itself, which few Virgos are adept at figuring out, until they've explored enough of who they *aren't* to get on with who they are.

When Virgo consciousness is *on,* it reveals where the rest of the universe is off. And when Virgo is *off* we all suffer, because this constellation encompasses more celestial real estate than any other. If the Daughter of Harvest wilts, Earth mourns and the underworld rumbles.

The journey of the sixth sign is a temple dance of devotion and desire, sometimes halting, sometimes stumbling, sinking into confusion, and rising to great heights of clarity where sudden flashes of meaning throw back the blackness like lightning, then recede, allowing the land to darken into rest again.

If a temple dancer catches you observing her, there may come a moment when she gazes into you with all the naked erotic force of a goddess. When Virgo is turned on, like the late summer sun emerging from behind the clouds, the slightest touch of that gaze can let you know you just passed some kind of test and have been admitted into the inner sanctum.

The tale of Persephone illustrates the wedding of appetite and wholeness. We bring the story to life each time we reenter the cycle of lovemaking with the raw innocence of a beautiful seduction, which in the heat of coupling raises deep hunger that can be satisfied by orgasm.

After your body is flushed clean, the stars and universe come rushing in. Like that feeling in a room when a baby is born, divinity arrives with a cleansing intimacy. As raw forces swirl, they birth new energies and create new life. When the flood recedes, it releases passion's hold, and the two who became one separate their bodies, but may keep harvesting together in astral fields.

VIRGO DRAGONHEAD/PISCES DRAGONTAIL

From the unconditional to the conditional

With Pisces behind you and Virgo ahead, you're departing from the unconditional and heading toward the conditional. This is the most exacting journey in the zodiac, with the most stringent demands, like passing a dragon through the eye of a needle. There's a way to live, a code to follow, a *feng shui* to practice, which can be found by becoming so true to your nature that you attune to the nature of all things. There's a purity in you dying to come out. If you push that with rigid dogma, it'll trap you, because you came to gain acute devotion more than anybody's ism. Like harnessing an ocean, this task is so monumental that sometimes all you can do is howl at the cosmic jest of having chosen to be human during a time of great chaos and confusion. Everything comes back to your body. Once your body leads you to the dance you were born to dance many things you thought were impossible fall into place, and, minus a few claw tips and shredded scales, your dragon emerges on the other side of the needle.

From the conditional to the unconditional

VIRGO DRAGONTAIL/PISCES DRAGONHEAD

With Virgo behind you and Pisces ahead, you're departing from the conditional and heading toward the unconditional. This is an orgy of surrender, sure to raise everything impossible to surrender to until you make love with it. So many thought forms block us from merging with the love we're made of, but are those shadow puppets real? Love and hate...Me and you...Reality and magic...These are thick coral reefs you bump into until their boundaries blur and colonies merge and you find yourself back where you started from. Incarnation is teaching you how to get out of your way by first seducing you through every possible variation of getting *in* your way. No matter how fervently you chase perfection you'll never get there, not because there's something wrong with you, but because the human part of you will always be human, even as the dragon in you soars like a dolphin leaping toward the sun, before it jackknifes, surrendering to gravity, and plunges back into the world ocean.

CHAPTER SEVEN

At the core of human being is a longing for companionship, the need to be seen and recognized, as well as the need to see and recognize others.

The great irony of our age is we're more connected to each other than ever while also more isolated. Shortly after waking in the morning many people register the comments of more individuals than many of our forebears interacted with in their entire lifetime. Yet, in terms of exchanging anything substantial, millions of lives are now poverty-stricken. To be constantly plugged in yet suffering lack of meaningful connection is a new development in human history.

Libra is the radiant one within you who longs to shine. It's the summons to rise above the shadow of lower nature and meet together in fields of splendor. It's the yearning to give and receive, know and be known, share life's beauties and burdens. Most of all, Libra is the craving for something rare in any time but probably even rarer now—authentic camaraderie.

The Secret Mirror
World of Libra:
The Art of Turning
Yourself On

YOU SAY *LEE*-BRA, I SAY *LIE*-BRA.

One hundred years ago the revolutionary Libran astrologer Marc Edmund Jones freed the zodiac from medieval trappings and updated it for the modern age. Prior to Jones and his apprentice Dane Rudhyar, a person's horoscope was read as if it depicted who they were. Jones and Rudhyar's great innovation was to read the birth chart not as if it portrays who you are but who you *might be*. Rather than treating the chart as literal fact, they envisioned it as the blueprint for a self-actualized human being. That move sprung astrology from a fixed determinant carved in stone to a celestial mandala spurring us to fulfill our unique individual potential.

These multi-talented visionaries (Jones was also a successful Hollywood screenwriter and Presbyterian minister, Rudhyar a novelist and composer whose work was performed by The Metropolitan Opera) were the teachers of my teacher, and they were obsessed with Libra. Toward the end of their lives they began to feel that the Neptune-in-Libra generation (born from 1944 to 1956) held the hope of humanity in its balance scales, by having enough passionate idealism to change the world.

But having the ability to do something and actually doing it are separate conditions that can be light years apart. Upon that gap hangs the destiny of this sign, and probably that of the human race.

Strongly influenced by those around it, Libra picks up the torch of its preceding neighbor, Virgo, to sort the difference between the real and the ideal, but aims the quest beyond the individual into the dyad.

This ultra-relational sign tends to fall madly in love with the ideal image of someone or something and get snockered by its charm, beauty, truth and illusion, which like the face of Helen of Troy can launch a thousand ships.

Thoughtful but impulsive, eager to share, frequently sidetracked, when Libra hearts get stolen it's not easy to know if they're heading toward a substantial likelihood or a mirage. It's not easy for Librans to know many things in fixed dependable ways, because their balance scales are always adjusting and readjusting.

Like the tailor of the zodiac, Librans spend life taking measure. The most important things they know, however, that really count, are rarely measurable, but flash by the Libra merry-go-round like gold rings waiting to be plucked while riding around the calliope on painted horses. Visions of beauty fly by with seductive invitations that remain just out of reach.

It'd be hard to find a more impassioned sign less in control of what it's doing, who somehow ends up precisely where it needs to most of the time, especially if someone else is sharing that painted saddle, because Libra is the magic of two.

Jones and Rudhyar called it *Lie-bra,* as it used to be called by many astrologers. They felt the long 'i' lifts the sign to full power, raising it to stand erect like the column of a temple, whereas *Lee-bra* is an Americanism that horizontally flattens the sign into the wheedley little mousy astrological stereotype of someone who can't make up their mind.

Though it'll feel awkward at first (it took me years), I invite you to pronounce the long 'i' if you read this chapter aloud (as the whole book may be vocalized for effect) or to hear it that way in your head.

Having guided thousands of individuals through the submerged topography of their inner nature since I created Soul Level Astrology in 1987, I can report from professional observation that everyone is much more than they seem and much more than they imagine, unless they've drunk enough ayahuasca, ingested enough LSD, or never done anything like that but have somehow gotten gobsmacked by what they're made of.

My clinical analysis after decades in the field: The universe inside you is no less astounding than the one outside, and if such a thing could be measured, might turn out to be the same size. You may not notice this by observing most Librans in your vicinity, though, because the secret world of Libra is so secret most Librans don't even know about it.

The seventh sign is a rogue's gallery of spiritual outlaws, consciousness-shakers, pie-in-the-sky dreamers, gossip-mongers, sexual acrobats, artists, diplomats, lovers, jugglers and fools; a magic looking glass; a telepathic switchboard of erotic interludes, which, like gazing at the sun, would fry your eyeballs if you beheld it straight-on. It creeps up on you with truths you think you perceive, only it turns out you'd just caught the rays bouncing off the foil packages those truths were wrapped in, till their wrappings melt and their thermodynamic core explodes its deeper meaning all over you.

$$\Omega$$

Like its glyph, Libra—which is the only non-breathing sign (symbolized by an object rather than living being)—has two distinct parts: the lower bar, which depicts the horizontal ground of the daily grind, the sturdy flatness of ordinary life, capped by the horseshoe-like dome of the upper bar, which invokes the sign's galloping leaps toward truth and beauty.

Being the only non-breathing sign suggests that the human part of Libra seeks a dynamic relationship with the non-human part: The raw primacy of emotion coursing through you seeks balance with high cosmic truths. Between the all-too-human struggle for personal happiness and the obligation to fulfill some higher ideal, Libra strives to attain balance.

Later, after Libran weights and measures give way to the following sign, the zodiac will dive into the scorpionic intensity of human being with an obsessiveness beyond that which Librans are prone to feel comfortable with. But until then, balancers can often be found following the call of some magic piper who's always just over the next hill.

The restless passion of Libra, as Jones and Rudhyar noted, is aching to free trapped consciousness and liberate pent-up spirit. But like stoic Lady Justice holding her balance scales, the sedate part of Libra strives to impassively stand for lofty notions and high ideals.

Inside each Libra, rationale wrestles with impulse, the raw tussles with the refined, hot emotion strives with cool detachment, and the need to push the river vies with the caution to stay dry well up on the bank. When Librans get in trouble it's either because they lean so far to one side they fall over, or because both sides attain such equal balance they produce stasis.

Though it may fuss and fume about it, Libra is usually better off with the irritation of imbalance than to have its scales settled too long, because excess balance can castrate or neuter the wild creativity out of this sign.

Rather than the smooth certainty of a predictable ride, the rough road is usually best for Libra because the bumps and potholes keep it on the edge of its seat. In the art of turning yourself on (as with other arts), an artist needs to stay wild inside. They need to keep their muse alive by honing an edge of divine dissatisfaction, continuing to challenge themselves and push boundaries of what's been done before and bringing something original to the table. If that edge is too sharp, Libra can turn cutting and abrasive, but if the edge is too dull they may sink into low-level or full-on depression, which can produce a near-lethal Libran paralysis of decision-making abilities in which their balance scales don't only settle down—they rust.

Like lovers and dreamers since time began, Libra desires the tentative blushing rose of young love—whether it's romance for a living being, creative project or cherished idea—to bloom perennially, but must balance that romantic vision with the realness of love's prickly thorns.

Just as the ram's thrust into being began the twelve-part journey of the zodiac, Libra's hunger for love and transformation begins the second half of the quest, where each sign will now become less enclosed in the personal sphere, more universal and complex.

At this first stage of the second half, the most basic unit of collectivity—the dyad—takes center stage, introducing relationship as a high art.

And in truth, if humanity is ever going to grow up, whether through the Neptune-in-Libra generation at long last fulfilling its promise or due to some similar miracle, it will result from us learning to master this art—because all around the world the old ways have become obsolete.

Society, at its most basic, comes down to you and me, which is the square root of civilization, a primal zone common to us all. If you inject novelty, adventure, desire and promise into the energy field between yourself and another, the whole world could change. At least your world could, which changes the part of the world that you are. And if you're a Libra that change is bound to spread because few signs are as irresistible as a turned-on Libra.

The seventh sign knows that underneath the drone of routine existence a universe is compacted in each of us like a clipper ship in a bottle. Until you free that ship your spirit remains corked, and the world views you as if behind glass: Authentic camaraderie is hard to find with anyone else till you find it with yourself, which means freeing the ship from the bottle.

Amidst today's constant electronic bombardment of content-free information, it requires radical awakening to realize normalcy *isn't*. It's not normal to live without passion, work a job that has no love in it, earn money doing something that drains your soul. It's not normal to swallow your dreams and squelch your creative giant who yearns to grab the reins of destiny and gallop beyond civilization's electric fences.

The Libran imagination, especially when young, is unrestrainable, launching dream after dream like magnificent sailing ships, which, if not boarded by others, may founder in the darkness and sink without a trace. But if someone bright and thirsty climbs aboard, Libran passion becomes a seductive-shipboard-multidimensional-tango.

Similar to how tales don't come fully alive till someone else is listening, the ecstatic spirit bottled up in the seventh sign gushes out like celestial champagne once someone pops the cork.

But if the magical side of Libra fails to be nurtured, this highly sensitive sign—not sensitive in terms of easily hurt, but sensitive to nuances and vibrations in its relational sphere—switches off each channel not being met, one by one, like a person switching off lights in every room of the house before turning in for the night.

For most children, regardless of Sun sign, the big shutdown happens between ages four and nine. If you catch Libra prior to then, you may get captivated by the zodiac's flashing little lighthouse of color, curiosity, charisma and desire.

If you find Libra in the following years, your main impression of them may lean more toward 'well-balanced' than ecstatically alive, because the same relational sensitivity that sweeps Libra into their psychic-emotive link with others shuts them down when they lower their vibration to match the low vibes of those around them.

Whether this melancholy tale arrives at a happy ending hinges on if Libra forms a relationship with someone or something who helps keep their magic alive.

Because balancers tend to get their lessons fast, that relationship doesn't necessarily have to be a long-term project. Sometimes even brief encounters yield long-lasting transformation for this ultra-relational sign.

Relationship provides the highest and lowest points of the Libra journey, capable of leading them as far from the happy ending they seek as it is of ushering them into it. It can take quite a few rounds on love's karmic rollercoaster for them to get dizzy enough to get off the ride and go somewhere where their head stops spinning long enough to tell the difference.

Getting along with others famously is something Librans excel at, making it essential for them to learn the difference between sunshine friends and all-weather companions. Often there has to be some betrayal of trust, real or imagined, for that to happen. What I owe you and you owe me is a constant Libran bone of contention, as is what's freely given and what must be paid for.

The seventh sign is built to pick up on what others are going through to the extent that it rarely operates in an independent zone, but in a telepathic relay station.

With not so much an absorptive as a highly reflective nature, many Libran actions (and inactions) are designed to compensate for the actions (or inactions) of those around it.

Most of these balance swivels occur involuntarily, as reflex action, but that might not be so bad, because becoming aware of interpersonal dynamics to the extent it's capable of can make Libra wonder if it's going batty, and trying to explain such dynamics to anyone not on LSD can be futile.

Authentic camaraderie is rare. Heavily compromised versions are more prevalent, because being brutally honest and candidly vulnerable with somebody else demands being that way with yourself.

Until you open a deep channel to yourself, you'll never get to the bottom of a relationship with anyone else. Nor the top. You'll get stranded in the middle, which is the bane of balancers. Your highs and lows will get trimmed to something safe and manageable, and a safe and manageable Libra may as well kill themselves quickly and get it over with, because that's what they're doing on the installment program.

I'm Libra. Starting with my first girlfriend at fourteen, most of my biggest changes and challenges have been delivered by lovers, but what an ordeal it has been to balance my ferocious need for freedom with my unquenchable desire to merge, and to counterweigh my need for stability with my commitment to transformation.

I've rarely felt I had the option to say no when love came calling, because some part of me knew it was the train to the future. I didn't know this consciously, especially when I first entered the railway, but I sensed that by myself I just wasn't going to make it to all the places I had to go. Like most teenagers I had only a vague idea of what those places were, but I could feel them calling.

I began most of my relationships smitten, courting the goddess with all the sacred lust and cosmic poetry I could muster, convinced this one would be my last, and I was devastated when it turned out not to be. Such ecstatic beginnings were etched in sharp contrast to the bad-acid blues that pitched me into a black hole when love ended and my world split apart.

After galloping through so many rapturous starts and catastrophic finishes, I couldn't help feeling that sooner or later the earnestness of my desire would melt the heart of some mighty goddess I must've gotten on the wrong side of in one life or other, so she could send me a love that lasted. So I never gave up and eventually mastered the brutal resurrective art of hauling myself out of dust and debris to start over. And over.

Growing up in a family unable to meet each other where it counts, I'd have many more missing pieces today, and be much more clueless as to my effects on others, if I hadn't found someone—many someones, as it turned out—to reflect back to me the versions of myself they saw, as I reflected them.

Looking back, I've come to feel that my parents and siblings were good people who sucked at intimacy. As a result I grew up craving connection. Then again, it might be that with all the Libra, Scorpio, Sagittarius and Capricorn in my chart, I would've been hot and horny and ultra-connective anyway, but maybe a little less obsessed.

Not every Libra pours themselves into love like I did. Some pour themselves into collaborations that thrive without the added bite of sex. Some pour themselves into art, crime or social work.

Throughout my love journey the most intense medicine I've had to swallow is the *truth in the mirror*. Each of my lovers exposed blind spots formerly beyond my awareness, places I'd hid from myself, things I hadn't been ready to see, until I began recognizing common themes in the wake-up calls the goddess kept sending me through her fetching human avatars. Eventually such telegrams began to penetrate the defenses of my stubborn male ego.

During an astrology session I conducted in 1992 in Carmel, California, a recently divorced client I'll call Maggie, who'd just ended her first post-divorce love affair, got exasperated about why an intelligent, honest and great-looking attorney like herself kept attracting men who messed around behind her back. I told her love's mirror was trying to get some important truth through to her.

She retorted heatedly, "What truth? Where's the fairness in that? I haven't lied or cheated! I haven't fucked anyone else. Though now I wish I had...."

"The truth in the reflection," I suggested, "may be that even though you never cheated anyone else, you've been cheating yourself. You sustained a marriage by ignoring the small voice warning you things were not the way they seemed. Love's mirror sent you partners who've been doing to you not what you've been doing to them, but *what you've been doing to yourself*. In that way it's a perfect reflection."

"Oh my Goddess—" she exclaimed, "you're right!"

A moment later she added, "Does that mean if I stop lying to myself, I'll stop falling for guys who lie?"

I told Maggie it was likely that would happen, and if it didn't, at least she'd be more inclined to spot the pattern sooner.

One reason I didn't give her a hundred-percent affirmative is because of the stepping-stone syndrome I discovered that occurs when a person emerges from long-term love, then gets into a hybrid relationship that has similarities with the old, mixed with something different.

One foot is planted on ground you're leaving behind, the other stepping toward something new. Stepping-stone loves don't always last, but they can take you halfway from where you used to be toward something more sustainable.

Even for people who've been on the path of consciousness for a long time, owning their reflection in the mirror is rarely easy. Maggie, who believed the universe gives you what you ask for, couldn't fathom why it would keep sending her losers, until she saw how badly she'd lost herself.

Similar to Maggie, I lost myself in love again and again but began to snap out of it in the early 1990s when a Santa Cruz therapist had me substitute the words *I, me* or *myself* for the name of the girlfriend who'd been tormenting me since our first date in the Santa Cruz Mountains two years earlier. That night, under the full moon, as we flirtatiously hiked through the forest, Alison began breaking up with me—before we ever got together! And she never stopped.

Why did I put up with that for two years?

As often happens in such frictional trysts, our carnal craving bypassed the entanglements of our egos to strip us down to jungle beasts who could never get enough sex.

Instead of moaning, "Alison's driving me crazy," I was advised by my therapist to say, "*I'm* driving me crazy." Instead of bitching, "I wish she would just fuckin' love me," I had to say, "I wish *I* would just love *myself*...." Instead of whining, "Why can't she commit to me?" I protested, "Why can't I commit to myself?"

Even though I tend to resist this kind of remedial behavior modification, after trying it on for months I began to realize the absurdity of how I'd always been conducting love.

Being Libran of course I couldn't resist applying the substitution to song lyrics: *Oh yeah I'll tell me something, I think I'll understand, When I say that something—I wanna hold my hand! I wanna hold my ha-a-a-and, I wanna hold my hand. And when I touch me I feel happy inside....* Though this example is meant to make you laugh it's interesting to speculate on how many love songs are really being sung by a singer to himself. To decode what many of us are really saying, remove the love object to expose the dialog between you and yourself.

As explosively transformative as my love affairs were, they could never take the place of my soul. It was heaven to make love with Alison but hell after, and it took me two years of hot sex and cold arguments to figure out what to do with that.

The Fast School of Love engages when we attract reruns of dysfunction to expose the dysfunction inside of us, and catch on to the lesson.

It's hard to see how you've been limiting yourself till someone limits you. It's hard to realize you've been betraying yourself till someone betrays you. Love's higher intelligence knows this, baiting you with a seductive someone who treats you the way you've been treating yourself, until you awaken to the truth in the mirror.

Without decoding her reflections, Maggie's loves didn't seem fair, and the pattern contradicted her spiritual understanding of the way things work. If everyone gets what they ask for, why would a faithful woman keep drawing unfaithful partners?

I tend to attract women who are either crazy about their freedom and, unwilling to surrender it, keep holding back from me, or who horn in on me till *I* pull away to preserve *my* freedom. Between chasing and being chased I spent decades on love's karmic merry-go-round.

Decoding messages your reflections send you can be sobering. And waking up to the messages you've been sending can be equally sobering.

After she divorced, Maggie eliminated the external source of her dysfunction without removing its internal taproot. Like a stalk of weeds yanked up, old relationship patterns tend to grow back with new partners till you dig up their roots.

At first it seemed the new man in Maggie's life had *nothing* to do with the old—at least that's what she was busy telling herself. When subtle signs crept in, she pushed them away.

Your partners are rarely aware of how they're reflecting you because they're caught in their own mirror.

I wasn't telling Maggie that her lovers decided to cheat on her because she was cheating herself. Their mirrors probably showed them a sexy affluent woman who they could sneak around. They probably thought they were getting away with something but didn't realize they were short-changing themselves by settling for cut-rate romance. To be real, love has to be honest. The deeper the trust, the farther relationship can go. Lacking deep trust, love can't go much of anywhere.

So even though those guys got away with extra-curricular activities, they robbed themselves and Maggie of love's greater riches, and may have been lost in their own mirrors even more than she was in hers, because Maggie eventually woke up to her reflections, and who knows if they did?

A relationship theme I discovered is the pendulum, where whatever you were most frustrated by with your last lover becomes the thing your next lover is most frustrated about with you.

Perhaps you spend years agonizing over your partner making time for everything but you. Then you split up, some creative project takes over, and you start a relationship with someone who gets dismayed by the amount of attention you're lavishing on the project. One day you're chagrinned to hear your former words come out of your new lover's lips. It seems the gods of love use poetic irony to restore karmic balance.

The Libra journey requires sorting out vital truths within multiple reflections. Sometimes the reflection is accurate but its magnitude needs to be adjusted. You might draw someone who keeps pushing away from you more extremely than you've been pushing away from yourself. Or you might attract a partner who's lying to you less than you're lying to yourself. In the latter case it can be harder to decipher the message, since human beings don't seem to learn their lessons till they're exaggerated.

Libra is like a hallucinogen, though a better word is entheogen, because hallucinating means seeing things that aren't there, whereas entheogens can dissolve conditioned forms of seeing to reveal the subtle dimensions that exist beyond.

Something in the nature of Libra thrusts open portholes to those dimensions, but because this sign is so attuned to thought forms around it, unless those openings are supported by others, they may remain unrecognized and close up.

Mind-expanding substances and significant others are two of Libra's three main looking glasses. The third is the mirror of art. Painting, sculpture, music, dance, literature, theater and film, if you dive all the way in, can launch you on a medicine journey of shamanic death and rebirth, as I've been launched upon by many works of art and during the four-year writing of this book. My ideas had to arise, die and resurrect many times on the keyboard, and I had to stumble into parts of the zodiac I didn't know existed.

As Libra awakens to truths in the mirror, it can be an ordeal to hold center and remain grounded. Its high reflectivity makes it one of the most complicated signs. Especially challenging is the Libra one-way mirror effect of *I see you so why don't you see me?*

This can be a situation agonizing and almost impossible to unpack, like the one I stumbled into at nine years old, when I realized I saw who my parents were more than they saw who I was. It was my first conscious revelation, and I don't think I've ever fully gotten over it. Like a card-carrying Libra, I am probably still compensating for that imbalance in ways I'm barely aware of.

Amidst its reflections and counter-reflections, balancing authentic camaraderie with authentic selfhood is something most Librans have to complete a great journey to achieve.

A good rule of thumb for this sign is when you think you've finally arrived at some dearly desired destination, don't be quick to celebrate, because you may be halfway there. Or less, and you will benefit more from a dose of humility, recommitment and retrenchment than premature self-congratulation.

Like its air-sign cousins Gemini and Aquarius, who similarly lavish much of their energy on analyzing, musing and deliberating, it can take a lot for this sign to learn the difference between thinking and doing.

No sign goes through as much identity crisis as Libra. None is as confused about selfhood and ego, or has a harder time sorting yours, mine and ours.

Like hyperactive kids, this sign loves to get carried away with the gushing enthusiasm of something it's bursting to share. Librans can get so wowed by their experience they fail to note when others are not so wowed. They think they're connecting amazingly with someone when they're mostly connecting with their own amazement.

Too much self-absorption in one phase can produce too much accommodation in the next. Many Librans push hard to one side then, like a rebounding Slinky, bounce to the other, then back to the first.... Through all the boinging, Libra can become a most impatient sign because few things happen quickly (or ideally) enough.

Above courts of law, Lady Justice presides over her balance scales blindfolded, but in matters of intimate companionship few of us remain impartial as all that. However, a large part of Libra is devoted to the fair and just, which can add overarching perspective when personal distortion sets in, but can also become, true to Libra's unique status as an object, overly objective, harsh, cold or judgmental.

When Libra is *on,* it cuts through superfluous rhetoric and entangled thought forms with a direct knowing that can be sudden and primal. Obscure designs in life and art reveal interconnecting themes that others miss and Librans spend hours marveling over. The presence of someone to share their marveling with can create whole new languages and secret trysts.

Codes and formulas, hidden passageways and arcane meanings delight Librans. Like the director of a play or movie, a Libran at the top of their game has a way of grasping not only individual performances but important underlying themes connecting various elements of the show. Seeing a thought-provoking movie or hearing a killer song sends the Libran mind scurrying through its psychic library of works with similar tones, patterns and resonances. I sometimes fantasize that the Library of Alexandria, the greatest collection of knowledge in the ancient world, didn't completely disappear from the universe but slipped into some Libran dimension where we can still gain access, deciphering the wisdom of the ages as we walk down the aisles. [8]

Such thematic unification equips Libra to see through life's surface plots to its grander organizational designs, but can also strand the sign in categorical thinking, one or more steps removed from flesh-and-blood engagement and real-world encounter. More than one of my previous lovers protested that I seemed more in love with love than with them, and they may have been right.

When Libra is *off,* this courtroom attorney of the zodiac tends to generate a cluster of rationalizations that obfuscate the issue and deny responsibility. The gasbagging logician in me must've confounded my

---

[8] In 300 BCE the Kings of Egypt had the brilliant idea to lure leading scholars, poets and scientists from many countries to Alexandria by offering them tax exemptions, free food and lodging and salaried life appointments to the growing library. At exorbitant cost the inheritance of Greek, Latin, Babylonian, Egyptian and Jewish cultures was assembled and archived. Such largesse generated not only books but high-level conversations and earthshaking discoveries. Euclid created geometry there. Archimedes discovered pi and laid the foundation for calculus. Alexandrian astronomers postulated a heliocentric solar system, with the Earth revolving around the Sun. Geometers proposed adding a leap day every four years to even out the 365 ¼ days that make up a year. Anatomists grasped that the brain and nervous system were a single unit. Engineers developed hydraulics, just to name a few; the full list is staggering. At its height the library contained half a million papyrus rolls that were organized by a new system that the first director of the library established: alphabetical order. (Many thanks to Stephen Greenblatt's *The Swerve,* for reopening these hallowed doors to give us a glimpse into ancient multiculturalism.)

poor mother during my high school years when, enhanced by one or two tightly rolled joints, I lawyered up on her to prove a point.

Instantaneous revelations and rapid-response rates keep Libran scales clanking up and down, Libran thoughts flying and Libran emotions whirling. Often Librans are the first to glimpse some impending drama moving through the shared psychic space, though, like many Libran sightings, it can be hard to determine if it's real or imagined, intentional or happenstance, and what, if anything, to do about it.

We all have all the signs within us in some unique blend. Each person is a one-of-a-kind admixture of the twelve-part art of being human, but the one most connected to the mix is Libra, because Libra is Blend itself.

The seventh sign is the mixing board of life. Like a sound engineer sliding faders, Libra goes through life adjusting the mix. And each adjustment affects the overall blend. If the bass guitar is too quiet, should you turn it up or turn the lead guitar down? And what does that do to the keyboards? If your companion just did something that piqued you, should you speak it or swallow it, and if you speak, what volume should you use? What tone? When is it better to hold the peace and when better to upend it in search of a greater harmony?

Libra has tremendous capacity to grow beyond its blind spots and rise to master its interactive art, but it's a funny art to master because how do you know when you've mastered relativity? How can you tell when someone's achieved *relationship*? What yardstick measures blend?

For a long time during the journey of the seventh sign the balance of self and other totters back and forth, as Libra underdoes and overdoes separation and union. But Libran happiness turns out to have less to do with manifesting perfect balance than with stabilizing the fulcrum at the base of the scales, which stands for firm solid presence here on Earth.

In love with ideas, negotiating checks and balances, modifying behavior in response to subtle cues, it can be a major event for Libra to simply show up.[9]

---

[9] One of Libra's great allies in this is Leo, who tends to be so unapologetically itself that it rescues Libra from the mirror maze of compound reflections. Similarly, Leo can be liberated by Libra's lucid objectivity, which can help overly subjective lions understand

For a sign built to run on revelations, particularly those pertaining to relationship, the big Libra shocker, sometimes forestalled for years, is—*you get to be yourself.*

The idea that you can be who you are may not sound earthshaking, but for Libra, becoming who you are is a prolonged ordeal through parts of you that reflect parts of others, parts of others that reflect parts of you, and parts of you that reflect nothing. Who you are amidst all these reflections is the greatest secret in the hall of mirrors.

When Libra stops looking to others for definition, and grounds into the full weight of its own experience, it gains a stable fulcrum. That defining moment occurs when you realize the outcome you've been frantically searching the world for is not what the world has to give you, but *what you already carry inside to give the world.*

This was the revelation I ended my first book with. That memoir tells the story of my mystical apprenticeship to a wild wizard in the Santa Cruz Mountains, and my misadventures through love and sex. Here are its final words:

> I realized then that being rich has nothing to do with the amount of money you have. You get rich the moment you recognize that you have so much more to give to this world than you'll ever need to take from it.

Upon this fulcrum the entire balance of Libra shifts, as you become astonished, mortified and chagrinned to learn you've been looking for others to provide something they never could've—the wholeness sleeping in your soul.

I didn't stabilize my fulcrum till my fifties, because in my quest for love, which I consciously began obsessing upon at age five, I leaned on relationship with superhuman strength, determined to complete myself

---

how they appear to others. Leo is the experience of being in the spotlight, Libra the view from the audience. Leo is *me*, Libra is *we*. Signs that are two signs away from each other on the wheel tend to work best together, though like all astrological truisms this can be offset by other factors.

by hooking up with the feminine, a strategy doomed to fail, though vital truths were contained in the illusion, and looking back, I wouldn't have had it any other way.

The illusion was that any woman could complete me. The truth was that every lover gave me a piece of myself. But until my fulcrum locked in place, until I came to trust and believe in myself as an independent being, until I learned to ground and center my energies so they weren't always hurtling toward the object of my obsession (and sequentially there were so many), I had a missing piece that no one else could fulfill, and my balance scales had a flimsy base.

Half the reason I spent fifty years trying to make love work was to avoid having to make *me* work. The other half was because I couldn't wait to get down with each delectable new goddess. The power of my sense memory is such that even now I can spend part of a day carried away by our carryings-on.

People born in the season of balance need good friends. They need barefoot time on the earth, massage, lots of fresh air, sex, aerobic exercise and sweat, strengthening their body to counter their frequent mind trips. Along with romantic and artistic revelations, the best Libran relief comes from sweaty, purging, physical-plane release like sports, dancing and music.

Libra is the premise that underneath life-as-is can be found giants of love, artists of the greater truths who express the ineffable so the rest of us might come close.

To live this sign to the fullest is to engage daily life as a workshop in wonder. The mundane flatness of the lower bar in the Libra glyph never touches but conjures the leaping arc of higher consciousness depicted by the upper bar.

If we use the straight bar as a diving board to sink the weight of incarnation of our fuller presence down upon, then we can spring like a swan into the mists of Lothlórien, into the shared vibration of all that's possible for awakened human beings.

Each moment, destiny asks us to dance, but most of us are too busy being who we think we're supposed to be to bother with becoming who we are. Each night the most luscious and erotic lover knocks on your door, offering you the juiciest encounter, but you have to stop making out with cell phones and algorithms long enough to open it.

The quest for truth and beauty has captivated artists since time immemorial. John Keats, though he wasn't a Libra, conjured the soul of the sign when he wrote a friend a few years before he died at twenty-nine:

> I am certain of nothing but of the holiness of the heart's affections and the truth of the imagination. What the imagination perceives as beauty must be truth—whether it existed before or not....

Whoa.

What the imagination perceives as beauty *must be truth*.

Whether it existed before or not....

That cuts through the mirror to the soul of this sign.

Mixed in with the rogue's gallery of characters you reflect and who reflect you on this side of the great divide are your past lives, ancestors, dream merchants, deceased friends and colorful cronies from the subtle dimensions you frequent on the other side.

Most of us are unaware of these subtle reflections, but that's not so much of a problem. It's a boon, really, because if you suddenly became aware of all the ultradimensional beings you traffic with, you'd disincarnate. You'd plunge into the live wire of the universe with no way back. So turning parts of yourself off is not always detrimental, though it's advisable to turn yourself off and on by intentional design rather than mass hypnosis.

A Grandmaster Ninja once told me the source of all power is balance, which reminds me of that famous quip of Archimedes, "Give me a lever long enough and a fulcrum on which to place it, and I shall move the world."

What if the purpose of human relationship is to compel each person to be utterly true to themselves?

What if seeing myself through your eyes can make me more *me*?

Can having made it this far into these pages be showing you parts of yourself that were always there but you didn't have a name for?

What if me incarnating more of my deeper self in order to be able to write this book (in other words, me becoming more *me*), instead of diminishing or taking away from you—as in the obsolete seesaw model of relationship, where one person rises at the other's expense—helps you become more *you*?

What if the profoundest achievement anyone can give the world is their authentic presence?

The ancient Libran Sufi master Rumi, who advanced human consciousness as much as anyone in the last 800 years, cried out:

Make us afraid of who we were!

Rumi doesn't humbly say, "Lord, help me transform" or "Show us a better way," because he knows the slippery slope of enlightenment. True to Libra, he's telling us that until we become more frightened of the person in the mirror than of the self we might someday be, we'll fail to awaken, a condition he calls playing the drum without taking the blanket off its head.

The Libra in me can't help running around the world pulling blankets off, which I guess is always what I've been doing. Long before I became an astrologer I was using poetry, sex and rap sessions to strip away coverings and get to the juicy stuff beneath.

When you become more afraid of who you used to be than who you might be, you tip the great Libran balance away from somnambulism toward the holiness of the heart's affections and the truth of imagination. With the ecstatic spirit of this highly contagious sign, you switch on channels that got switched off, discarding blankets and releasing the trapped ships of humanity to sail free.

LIBRA DRAGONHEAD/ARIES DRAGONTAIL

From the simple to the complicated

With Aries behind you and Libra ahead, you're departing from the simple and heading toward the complicated. In earlier lives you saw most things entirely through your own eyes while missing the views of others. You got so caught up in your own track you couldn't tell if it was veering toward or away from someone else's, which limited your empathy and understanding. This time around you're developing clairsentience, which, similar to clairvoyance (which is psychic vision) and clairaudience (psychic hearing), enables you to sense what others are experiencing without needing to be told. The more you care about someone, the sharper this sense grows. It takes lots of back-and-forth to master it. Going too far can unbalance you by becoming so inundated with the other person's experience you lose track of your own. Not going far enough risks chasing your tail by repeating past-life self-enclosure. Your dragon is flying out of a narrow past toward the shared world that manifests when two get together heart to heart and soul to soul. If you're in one of those shared worlds, put your ear to the ground and learn to listen. If you're not and want to be, put your ear to the ground and listen anyway, because that world is busy being born in you the same time it's being born in the person you're going to share it with as soon as you're both ready to find each other.

From
the complicated to
the simple

LIBRA DRAGONTAIL/ARIES DRAGONHEAD

With Libra behind you and Aries ahead, you're departing from the complicated and heading toward the simple. Beware second-guessing. Trust your gut. Pondering comes naturally to you because you got good at it in an earlier life, but don't linger there, or you'll stumble around a clockface of past-life footprints. Direct engagement is what you came back for. You have to engage more than your mind, though, and dive off the clock into strong subtle energies that usher you forward. That dive streamlines your ride through the physical plane, bypassing convoluted thought webs that trap the free movement of individuals. As quick as thought travels, energy travels quicker. Underneath the complexities of our time, the spirit of the species is fuming to bust loose, and Aries leads the charge. Thoughts can carry human consciousness into the future, but energy links your subtle senses to life-enhancing forces of the present. Your dragon is stalking evolutionary breakthroughs you might not find with your mind, but they can be identified by the tingling in the forearms of the dowser in you.

CHAPTER EIGHT

Scorpio is haunted.

Scorpio is haunted by everything that hasn't happened yet.

Scorpio's haunted by every time it failed to show up as the giant of love it is, every time it shrank in the shadows. Scorpio's haunted by every passion it has had to squelch and truth it's had to swallow.

Like a once-thriving country decimated by partisan feuds, the spirit of the sign has gone underground, reduced to clandestine activity, behind closed doors, tossing and turning at 3 a.m.—the hour the soul is said to be farthest from the body—when others are oblivious.

Fighting to see clearly through bleary-eyed insomnia, Scorpio can no longer ignore the suspicion gnawing away at it: Somebody has taken over its life. Somebody is wearing its clothes, sleeping in its bed, making love to its mate. Someone is eating its food and breathing its air. The situation has become so extreme that only extreme action can remedy it. Having run out of other options, Scorpio finally admits to itself the only solution left is suicide.

The Magnificent Death of Scorpio: The Art of Obsession

INSTEAD OF BEING TAUGHT TO FEEL THE FULL EXTENT OF WHAT we feel, we're trained to ignore intense feelings, polish our ego and join *The Show*. We're taught to meet each other out on the surface where Appearance is king and Actuality is the stinking peasant who gets pushed aside and forgotten. We're taught to ignore the dead elephant in the living room and replace our true nature with a substitute, whom we send to join the other substitutes that keep the world running. It's this changeling that Scorpio must find a way to bring down. It's its artificial self whom Scorpio has to kill.

The compromised state of Scorpio is similar to the compromised state of other signs, except few others take it so personally, feel it raking their gut, are driven insane by the saneness of it all, which keeps this sign tossing and turning through the long night.

It's the nature of scorpions to crawl through the darkness to get to the light, as one did more than 400 million years ago, when, venturing out of the Devonian sea, it became the first Earth creature to walk on dry land.

Deep in your reptile brain, you're still making that morphogenetic trek out of the slime at the bottom of the gene pool. Down in the primal ooze you're a creeping scorpion, a feral hunter, an abandoned child, a sex-starved horndog, a savage veteran of man's inhumanity to man, where the most casual glance might provoke mayhem or murder.

There's nothing terribly strange about any of this, and nothing particularly wrong—so long as you don't deny, demonize, project it onto others or violently act it out.

Some of your primal truths may not feel good. Maybe none of them feel good, but what's good about this part of you, what's great and miraculous about it—is that it's *real.*

Beyond the glad-handing of fair-weather friends, the water-cooler intrigues of office politics and cute emoticons of social media, your primal truths supply indisputable evidence of your *aliveness.* They prove you exist. They burn like hydrochloric acid through the corrosive half-life that's taken over the world, where your madness is your best chance of being sane.

If you penetrate the layers of resistance and denial that form the innermost defenses of ego, you'll enter the lair of the scorpion. If you immerse yourself in its dark tonic, open your pores and let deep truths all the way in, you can become so present at bottom that you'll learn what you're made of and what we all are made of—for we all trudged out of the slime with that first scorpion.

Until Scorpio awakens to the nest of primal truths crawling inside it, each place it goes is another hideout, and every move it makes is buying time.

Regardless of your Sun sign, beneath your cultured airs are your Scorpio parts, which contain a poisonous stinger that can do something more sophisticated parts of you cannot: Assassinate the artificial self.

Like a demolition crew of one, Scorpio is the wrecking ball of the zodiac, swinging the great weight of truth back and forth to obliterate the falseness of cover stories, especially the stories we don't think of as stories—we just think of as the way things are.

When you catch yourself thinking things are a certain way, and *only* that way, and *always* that way, chances are you've caught a scorpion by the tail.

There might be a way things are for a moment, but Earth isn't even in that place anymore, the galaxy moved, and you've lost and gained millions of molecules since then.

When you latch onto personal myths of *the-way-it-is* vintage, you're getting hooked by tales that come from elsewhere than the soul, because your soul knows better. Your soul is filled with possibilities galore, which it'll get busy with the moment your ego stops plastering the universe with stories.

If the zodiac were music, Scorpio would be opera: clashing forces surging to trap lightning, fend off rivals, conquer the gods and live forever. When calmness arrives, it supercharges the silence, because you don't know which direction the angels are coming from and whether they're going to usher you into paradise or slaughter you.

Don't be deceived by the stoic demeanor of many Scorpios. Don't get fooled by the lackadaisical presentation of anyone around you, because the most inconspicuous person contains operatic forces if you look deep enough, and you have to look very deep to get to the soul of this sign—for Scorpio is soul itself.

Though it contradicts the understandable but nihilistic modern idea that Earth would be better off without humanity, my Scorpio instincts can't help feeling that's terribly wrong. I believe the soul of our planet is crying for the soul of humanity to come all the way in and crack the skin of our substitute like a molting scorpion, so Earth and humanity can get beyond flirting and consummate their ancient unrequited love affair, releasing the deep passion they have for each other.

The Scorpio path leads down and in before it leads up and out. Scorpio gains resurrection through gravity, for when we penetrate the facile surface of what *isn't*, we enter the nucleating core of what is. I see that core as a ruby heart whose laser beams blast holes in the architecture of denial.

Long after midnight, one steamy summer night in the early 1990s, drunk in New Orleans, after sitting in on percussion with a zydeco band in the French Quarter, I walked deserted streets alone, with my drum in a black case strapped over my shoulder, my water bottle clanking against it, while a few blocks away someone was getting murdered.

I didn't know about the murder while I made my way across empty streetcar tracks, past wrought-iron fences, tall oaks with Spanish moss and shaggy lawns on the long walk back to the apartment where I was staying. I also didn't know two other people had been recently killed in that part of town.

I did notice, though, an eerie absence of other pedestrians, as if I were the only one left on Earth, apart from some fearsomely large rats darting through the shadows. And I noticed an odd traffic response, where the three or four cars that passed—which seemed strangely few even at that hour—gave me wide berth, swerving as far from me as possible.

The next day when I learned of the killings, I realized people in those cars had probably known of them and, assuming only a maniac would be out then, couldn't get away from me fast enough.

That night as I walked under the streetlights I was hit by the most putrid stench I'd ever smelled, which seemed darkly familiar, like vapors rising from the bathroom of a skanky bar, or toxic stink from a freshly used abattoir, but I couldn't identify the source till I squatted and found it wafting up from the sewer.

I realized that underneath the music we'd played, which had gotten people dancing in the street, underneath the storm drains I'd passed, maybe since I'd arrived in New Orleans two days earlier, that stink had been festering.

As vile as it was, it was a relief to track what had been haunting the periphery of my awareness to its lair. I sniffed one emetic sting of rancid seafood, cat piss, rat corpse, blood and condoms, which induced me to vomit, and as I did I flashed on New Orleans as the root chakra of the nation, where everything swallowed by mass consciousness eventually sluices down to its fetid bowels.

After, I stood and rinsed my mouth with the remaining water from my bottle, spat it out and continued.

Like the New Orleans Stink, parts of you and me are so intense as not to be believed.

But so it is with all of us, so it has been since the dawn of time. And the worst of the worst—whatever *that* is—has the power to shock you awake, if you're bold or crazy enough to stay with it long enough to get defibrillator*ed* by it.

In the animal world, scorpion eyes don't see like yours and mine. They don't perceive objects in sharp focus, but blurrily. However, they're among the most light-sensitive on the planet, to the extent that some of the 2,000 varieties of scorpion navigate solely by starlight. Imagine arachnid eyes so cosmically receptive that a creature barely off the ground finds its way by the constellations....

When you enter the realm of the scorpion, darkness fills with light. In that blurry cave, where every star is a ghost and every ghost carries a star, it's not possible to understand why you feel what you feel.

The great power of the eighth sign doesn't arise from rationalizations. Scorpio's obsession is not to rationalize, debate or explain, because those are easily coopted by ego, and the zodiac's most ancient inhabitant isn't trying to convince anybody of anything. Scorpio's obsession is to *be*.

Of every creature that populates the zodiac, the one who knows the deep secret of being is the smallest and most poisonous: to become blazingly alive you must pull off a glorious death. To be born into everything you *are,* you must die to everything you're *not*.

Marooned in society's rampant non-being, the only way to pull off such an Olympian feat is to get ultra-real with the most unbearable parts of yourself, get ultra-real with the most intense parts of others, and get ultra-real especially with anything you love and anything that gets in the way of what you love.

In a terrarium at the San Francisco Zoo I watched scorpions scurry about, lit by ultraviolet beams that activated their blue-green fluorescence. Like glowing phantoms they flickered in and out of sight, as if materializing off a DayGlo poster from a blacklight room on an acid trip in a 1960s head shop. I felt stoned just from watching and had a hard time tearing myself away.

It was there I learned that the sting of some scorpions contains an entheogen that sends their victims shucking off their mortal coils while tripping their brains out. Not a bad way to go.[10]

---

[10] Aldous Huxley, though he was a Leo, who wrote *The Doors of Perception* about his 1953 mescaline trip, ten years later chose to go out tripping on the LSD his wife brought to the hospital where he died.

Apart from Leo, Scorpio is the only zodiac sign whose constellation looks even remotely like what it's supposed to in the night sky. In the continental US the scorpion prowls so low in the south that its bottommost section often drops below the horizon, leaving the upper end of its curled stinger exposed and ready to strike, as the predator lurks around the dark rim of autumn. The long spread of its celestial outline reminds me that scorpions were once bigger than lions, and makes me shudder.

Further up its body, red Antares, one of the brightest stars in the sky, burns like a ruby dot marking the heart of the scorpion. In the terrarium I saw tiny beating hearts of translucent scorpions mark their bodies with similar dots, and was struck by how the little critters beneath me resembled the god-sized one above.

I also learned scorpions dance upright clasping each other's claws while mating, and birth as many as a hundred live young, who climb two-by-two on mama's back, where she protects them till they care for themselves. As fearsome as a scorpioness may appear, it's good to recall she's somebody's loving mother.

Wherever people meet, there's the way things seem and the way they *are*. We create an exoskeletal encasement of ego to protect the raw beating heart of what we feel.

Most human interaction occurs way up on the surface. Most of us have forgotten how to sustain a vital existence down below. Many people are unaware there *is* a down below. If you're dancing your life away in a social adaptation waltz, realness, by comparison, can seem psychedelic.

Scorpio is what makes us human. It's where we come from. It's who we are, beneath everything else we are. The sex-starved horndog in you gives you oomph for another go at life, another shot at glory. The abandoned child in you offers empathy for a species in exile, far from the love where it belongs. The seasoned veteran of humanity's karmic battles with itself gives you grit and moxie to stand firm against rampant floods of ignorance. Facing everything you feel is the only way to restore truth and wholeness to a species killing itself off for lack of them.

The disowned truths it takes to keep the machinery of civilization going drain beneath collective consciousness into subterranean caverns we could call Scorpio. The misty funk the eighth sign frequently goes in and out of has to do with its ability to pick up on things others put down. It takes a long while for such deep truths to percolate in the dark places Scorpio must sit with in order to learn how to die.

Down in the dark it's not easy to tell one thing from another. In the bottom of the psyche, which is this sign's natural habitat, the roots of all things intertwine. Like a scorpion with blurry vision, it's difficult for this sign to distinguish its stuff from everybody's stuff.

When the first scorpion emerged from the sea, it wasn't just acting on its own behalf but setting the direction for much of what was to come. More than any other sign, except perhaps Aquarius, the scorpion was born knowing the truth of what the great soul singer Solomon Burke sang: *If one of us is chained none of us are free....*

Like a mama scorpion, there's a lot riding on the back of this sign, some of which can be understood by the significance of its position relative to the twelve. In the first half of the zodiac, individuality establishes itself. In the second half, individuality transcends itself, as the narrow drive of the personal gives way to the vast waters of the universal, like Scorpio heading toward Pisces, or a river fighting its banks on the way to the sea.

Even though Scorpio isn't the end of the zodiac, it's the end of the personal drive at its purest, because from now on the journey must begin linking to greater and greater forces. Though the significance of the individual will never entirely disappear from the picture, after Scorpio it'll fade into the background, as more transcendent energies, which only emerged in dribs and drabs thus far, step out to command the stage.

But Scorpio can't transcend the personal till fully doing justice to it. By uncovering primal truths, Scorpio learns to live close to itself. Down there we're creatures of pure experience. No sophisticated reasoning; we can only feel, and though it can't possibly identify the full extent and power of what it feels, Scorpio feels more than any other sign except perhaps Pisces.

Such bottom dwelling grants the sign a ring of authority, which allows it to be recognized by those willing to go the distance, who sense that when all else fails, Scorpions are the ones with the backs you can cling to and ride on.

Like a saltwater marsh at low tide, Scorpio is the mucky origin of the psychic food chain that sustains the soul of the species. Everything stinky that no one wants to deal with breeds in its mire. To build another housing development, wetlands can be drained without immediate drastic consequences, but if all wetlands were drained and the air above them turned sweet as perfume, human life on Earth would probably end, though our poisonous little predator might find a way to go on.

Wherever there's no room for inconvenient truths there's little place for this eldest member of the zodiac, who possesses the secret of reincarnation, because scorpions have had to regenerate themselves many times during 400 million years of catastrophic extinctions.

It's the lowly and much-maligned scorpion we should thank for exporting life out of the primordial ocean and conveying it beyond so many species who entered and exited the world stage while it crawled past booming volcanoes, continent-carving glaciers, cataclysmic floods, broiling famines and explosive meteor crashes, to become one of the greatest success stories on the planet.

Scorpions managed this so well they now flourish on every continent except Antarctica. From a scorpion's point of view, humanity, having arrived a paltry 200,000 years ago, probably seems like the new kid on the block, who nobody will know what it is really made of for a few hundred million years or so.

Without the tendency to feel too much and go too far, Scorpio would lose its vital force, because over the eons just about everything on the planet has changed more than it has. Anything external you put your faith in is transitory; only the realness of soul can produce an antidote for the unreality of our time.

One of the great truths in the depths is that everyone's broken. Everyone's broken and society's even more broken. When you stop denying brokenness, you learn to see in the dark, where, below slick appearance, cool contrivance and mass denial, everyone is love-hungry and truth-starved.

The recovery of our species from its current existential dilemma can be prodded by the recognition that to be broken is not an abnormal condition that must be coffined up in guilt and shame, but just the price of incarnation. Beneath the skin we're primitive creatures slithering through the mud, carrying angels. The moment we stop denying hurt it begins to heal.

The path of the scorpion isn't for the fainthearted, because it demands attachment, surrender and release, again and again, till you're stripped clean of everything but soul. Only by dying many times can we rise from the ashes for one more chance at love and wholeness. Someone has to hold humanity's feet to the fire, and Scorpio has those intractable claws....

> *whisper to the flame:*
>
> *take me*
> *break me*
> *scrape everything but God off me*
>
> *let me come naked unto this house of fire*
>
> *burn the knowing out of me*
> *and fill me with love that's not love of but just love*
> *just love*
> *just love*

Creating a magnificent death demands increasing your attachment while releasing your expectations, the kind of superhuman challenge that can bring out the best in this sign. Which means trusting your obsession enough to follow where it leads, while knowing that path may conclude other than planned. Love, when it finally arrives, may look entirely different than you thought.

If you feed your desire while starving your expectations, you'll be reborn in the deep. To pull that off, Scorpio has to go through a lot of hell to get to a little bit of heaven.

Don't get me wrong: It's not that you're supposed to always smell vile stenches and think horrific thoughts, it's just that you need to feel whatever it is you're feeling, which is the only way to get past it. The Scorpio code is: Whatever doesn't kill you makes you strong—*and whatever kills you makes you stronger.*

If you start by being realest in the heaviest places, anything else you have to deal with is bound to be lighter.

There's no need to prolong suffering. I do not advocate martyrdom. No hell need linger longer than it has to. Despite its reputation, Scorpio isn't a morbid sign. Scorpio isn't hung up on death. Scorpio isn't even hung up on sex.

Scorpio's hung up on being *alive,* and sick to death of everything half-alive, which is why it keeps going and going. The reason to dive into hell isn't to stay there but to grab what you need and get out.

One warning: It's the nature of the sign to trespass commonly-agreed-upon boundaries and break taboo, which will generate static in the collective jumbotron.

Someone who's gone to hell and back becomes a moving target for others to project their disowned shadow on. That's a hell of an obstacle course to have to go through after you've just returned from fighting your own demons and now have to tackle other people's, because they're not dealing with them, and what's worse—blaming you.

Scorpio is the silent saboteur sent to disrupt the status quo, the dark stranger, the dangerous outlaw, seething with so many supercharged forces that the moment it steps out in the open and reveals itself it's in peril.

What an awesome thing to have one sign willing to go farther than the rest, but that one needs backup and protection, because, as formidable as Scorpios are they're also psychic sponges who can't help absorbing the disowned emotions leaking out of other people's psyches, flooding the ground all around them.

In the mystery school in a cottage under the Redwoods I stumbled into as a young man (which I wrote of in *2012: Crossing the Bridge to the Future,* soon to be republished as *Love, Sex & Astrology*), after class one evening I found myself alone with my teachers William and Sara, a rare situation I relished. William spoke for the first time of the *egregore* (pronounced egg' gree gore), which occult thought recognizes as a destructive entity that arises when a group of people get together and think the same thoughts.

In the egregore, psychic manifestations of group thought forms are said to take on a shadow life, as a vampiric organism that feeds on disowned desires and repressed thoughts, and acts out the negative side of group intention.

Possession by the egregore has the exasperating quality of making anyone who speaks out about the situation seem as though they're the one causing such toxic negativity, rather than just exposing it, in an occult version of kill-the-messenger.

I think William was warning me to be on the lookout for such a collective organism growing out of our own group, which had recently formed around him. He may not have known he was warning me, though. Eventually something like this did come to pass, but that's a story for another time.

I think world consciousness has gotten so twisted it has spawned an egregore who's devouring the planet and sucking the soul of the species dry. To vanquish such a monster we've got to get awfully real now, so need Scorpio more than ever.

Whereas the previous sign Libra reached out to clear the field of relationship of false reflection, Scorpio fights society's taboo against knowing yourself, which cuts deeper than the taboo against knowing someone else.

To go your own way against prevailing currents in the contemporary cultural puritanism and witch hunts you need thick skin and x-ray vision, which penetrates the body of collective denial like invading bacteria. Forces of shame and blame can swarm the bacteria like white blood cells, making you seem to be the one causing the problem, which can make you feel delusional and begin to doubt yourself, begin to feel shabby and isolated and no longer sure you know what you know.

Without trusting its instincts Scorpio has little to go on, because it's the most instinctual member of the zodiac, who operates largely by feel, like a blind scorpion crawling through a cave, registering every vibration to distinguish predator from prey.

Scorpio lacks the elaborate pretense of some other signs, or perhaps just can't be bothered with it. Like a predator out to devour artifice, it's as if they have to save their energy for what's essential, since predators only have enough energy to stalk prey so many times before collapsing.

Whatever sign you are, until you complete the journey of the scorpion your higher aspirations remain castles made of sand.

More than Scorpio thinks, it *feels*.

More than Scorpio conjectures, it *wants*.

Scorpio has deep wants.

And to each want, Scorpio must learn to say *Inshallah: If Spirit wills it...* Inshallah, or to put it another way: *Trust God but keep your camel tied....*

The quest of the scorpion is to follow the ways of desire, but carefully. Don't let anyone talk you out of what you're obsessed with, because your obsession may prove realer than many things you thought were real. Honor your obsession, but equally honor the fact it may never happen, or might happen much differently than you think.

Sex and death are usually associated with this sign. Few people have made peace with or gotten to the bottom of either, and fewer still have made peace with or gotten to the bottom of both, which is a sorry state of affairs here on planet Earth, because they're the bookends of life. Sex begins our journey through the physical plane and death ends it. If we remain this ignorant of both ends, how will we ever grasp the truth of anything in between?

Regarding death, the way you used to be, even a moment ago, no longer exists. That person is dead, though someone else in you is newly arrived. The relationship you had with your lover ended yesterday because neither of you are the same today. All things are in a constant state of birth, death and decay. When you stop trying to control the process and merge with it, you cut loose from the psychic herd dogs society uses to keep evolutionary mutation from breaking out.

So many people fear the loss of youth and the encroachment of death that billions of dollars are made milking that paranoia into Botox, breast lifts, tummy tucks and other attempts at cosmetic immortality. But the realness of death and aging, like the realness of orgasm, packs a sting that can jerk you out of the trance of normalcy.

The passion of the scorpion is to meld things that have been dying to find each other: Scorpio is fusion. The Scorpio physics of fusion state that if you want something bad enough (or good enough) you should crank up your want till it creates a vacuum in the shape of that want, which nature abhors, and so will fill that space with what you desire, though it may take much longer than you expect, possibly even lifetimes, though what's one lifetime or two to a scorpion?

Consecrating desire contradicts popular spiritual advice to outgrow attachment and rise above material wants, to which my four Scorpio planets say *bullshit*. If you didn't want to get attached, why would your soul have taken a body? If Scorpio didn't need to grasp and hold, why would it have two mammoth pincer claws?

The path of obsession, admittedly, can be too hot to handle, and isn't the only path through the zodiac. But until you free yourself to feel what you feel, know what you know, and need what you need, your claws will snap shut on thin air and fail to grasp that one true life David Whyte talks about.

After you depart this body and return to spirit you can have all the transcendence you want, but while you're here you may as well be all the way here. Until Scorpio follows its obsession to its glorious or bitter end, the four remaining signs will be less able to grow beyond this critical stage and do justice to the cosmic mysteries that arise in the final stretch of the zodiac.

I see Judaism as a Scorpionic religion, because its mystical book, *The Kabbalah,* relates that *In the Beginning was Yahweh,* and in its utter aloneness, *Yahweh* withdrew its vast life force into its innermost recesses, like a neutron star spawning from the collapsed core of a supergiant.

Yahweh's withdrawal created a void outside itself, which in one colossal tsunami, the universe rushed in to fill. Creation born from contraction. Existence summoned from restraint.

Scorpio is whatever you can't live without. It's the cleansing catharsis of sexual union and stark perseverance in the face of ridicule and scorn. It's the deepest chamber of self-confrontation and the craving of estranged lovers to reunite. It's humanity's search for wholeness. How multitudes can thrive on superficial existence while such great and towering love remains unclaimed is something the Scorpio parts of us will never understand.

The soul inside the awakening child takes a good look at the world and says:

> My mother is not who she is.
> My neighbors are not who they seem.
> We are not who we're supposed to be.
> I came for love but love isn't happening, so I'll put my real life on hold in favor of the next best option, which is to construct some verisimilitude that can carry me through:
> I'll create a changeling.

Living without love and wholeness is the full-time job everyone's employed in but no one's talking about. As if the world really were the way it looks on TV game shows and steamship cruises. Inside this virtual reality, our inner nature suffers cramps of stagnated love, while the canned laughter goes on and on.

Obsession, freed from expectation, can turn you into a superhero with the compassion of Quan Yin and strength of the Incredible Hulk. Scorpio's genius is to gain liberation via obsession (unlike the zodiac's other revolutionary, a few signs down the road, Aquarius, who seeks liberation from nonattachment).

If you become sexually free in the most genuine way, your sex life probably won't fit the picture most people imagine. Sexual freedom has little to do with the number of lovers you have or fancy positions you pull off. It has little to do with how many people think you're hot.

Sexual freedom arises when you come alive inside and feel everything you feel. It arises when the *shakti* (primal life force) in your body meets no resistance in the outlets it uses to stream into someone else, and when the strong force of desire in someone else meets no resistance streaming into you. Sexual freedom occurs when your heart opens and keeps you as vibrantly present to your lover's experience as to your own.

Scorpio isn't after sex so much as *fusion,* which comes down to whether you're still holding something against yourself. Or against God, the patriarchy, your mate or the kid who beat you up in fourth grade: *Anything you hold against anyone, you're holding against yourself.* When you release the grudge you've been nursing with existence, you expunge your system of psychic and physiological toxins and begin to make your way back from the dead.

Salvaging deep truths is the primary initiation on the Scorpio journey, but for every depth dive Scorpio completes, it has to undergo a secondary initiation when bringing the fruits of that dive to others.

When you contact the soul, you contact blinding radiance. Compared to that light, much of the world looks dim. Love on the inside will produce many challenges on the outside to teach you how to carry it. Wholeness you find down under gets fractionated on the surface, where you'll be tested to keep embodying what you found, keep extracting truth from untruth and health from toxicity.

Life naked, raw and direct, without the deflecting mediation of the changeling, is often intense, sometimes brutal, but always real. No longer haunted by what hasn't happened, no longer tossing and turning through the long night, no longer exhausted by pushing ghosts away, the magnificent death of Scorpio leads it straight through the heart of darkness to become *the most loving sign of all.* With Scorpio when you get stuck, inject love into the fear and push all the way through that death to get to the regeneration. You'll know you've gotten there when everything you've ever had to go through becomes so much more than worth it.

SCORPIO DRAGONHEAD/TAURUS DRAGONTAIL

From innocence to obsession

With Taurus behind you and Scorpio ahead, you're departing from innocence and heading toward obsession. The purity of childhood holds a dear place in your heart, as a fond refuge that beckons when invasive forces intrude. But beyond that shelter your dragon is calling, and its way is rough and raw but realer than every other. You were born to claim truths that can't be won by concession and compromise. If someone tells you to tame down, you're too intense, too obsessed, too *much,* they're correct—you're far too much for everything that's not enough, but exactly right to dig your claws into the farce that has turned a planetful of dragons into herd animals. You're a warrior of love who's not here to tippytoe through social niceties, but to fan your wings whipping up a wind that sweeps the underworld clean. Depending on your chosen field, you may or may not wish to draw attention to this, but operate undercover like a spiritual outlaw, stealing complacency and replacing it with passion. Like a scorpion or dragon, you'll have to molt every so often, so don't get too attached to anything but love.

From obsession to innocence

SCORPIO DRAGONTAIL/TAURUS DRAGONHEAD

With Scorpio behind you and Taurus ahead, you're departing from obsession and heading toward innocence. Your soul's been scurrying like a scorpion through reincarnational tunnels that demanded obsession with the basics and little room for anything else. Such rawness gave you x-ray vision, supercharged your survival instincts and revealed skeletons in many closets. Despite all that, you've come back to swing on lamp posts and dance jigs in mausoleums. Your willingness to emerge from the karmic tunnel is being sorely tested, summoning you to gain a faith that moves mountains. When you're aware of the odds against love prevailing and bet everything on it anyway, your dragon digs deep into the garden of life with an innocence that can make the sun rise. It's easy for the naive among us to be innocent, but you signed up for something harder: a chance for the veteran soul to become young again, not by being gullible and easily duped, but by resurrecting a sense of wonder so deep it can't be denied.

CHAPTER NINE

No synchronicity is incidental, so far as I can see, and my Sagittarian Moon may be the farthest-seeing part of me. Maybe it's more accurate to say 'farthest-sensing' because I believe Sagittarius senses much more than it sees. The rest of me probably spends a lot of time catching up to what my Saj Moon knows.[11]

Your Moon, which has a lot to do with how you feel things, is the key planetary influence in childhood, especially in early childhood when you're bombarded by sensations and life is more dreamy than awake. During the rest of your life as other parts of you awaken, the Moon's domination subsides, unless other factors amplify your Moon more than normal.

I have Saj Rising, with Moon on my ascendent, which expands the lunar influence throughout the course of my life, so I never quite leave childhood behind. I never fully grow up. As you might imagine, this has its ups and downs....

The Sagittarian part of you is a dreamer, whose coming-out party is otherwise known as adolescence. That's when dreams begin to take flight, and either set the direction of your adult life in motion, or sputter and flop and get overruled by external factors like parental pressure and cultural conformity. If your dreams sputter and flop, they may or may not regain flight altitude during the rest of this incarnation, which your soul crash-landed into like a centaur who lost its wings.

Few of us are fully equipped for the rigors of incarnation when we arrive. Few of us are fully prepared to deal with sex and death, websites and traffic jams, because

---

[11] Even though Sagittarius is spelled with a 'g', when abbreviating I use a 'j' to distinguish the soft 'g' sound from the hard. Thanks to California astrologer Bill Strider for this.

we've just come from the oneness and glory of spirit into the mundaneness and madness of matter, during a time of great confusion.

Compared to your body of light, your physical body is a clunky centaur stranded on the wrong side of paradise. The most we can do is charge in and hope for the best, because around here it's never gonna be like it was over there. No one's always a gazelle on this side of the great divide, where we keep tripping over our own feet, and any gazelle-ness is likely to be followed by incarnational splatters.

The ninth sign is wild about freedom. Moving just to move can easily occupy the first half of a Sagittarian life, and then some. For me it's never stopped, this sense of wandering, as if I'm an unfinished symphony rather than a polished stone.

Life for Sagittarius is like eternal adolescence, when you're stranded on a precipice between everything that's come before and all that's yet to be, yearning for wings. Puberty, enflaming your hormones, has you jumping out of your skin. Soon as you think you're on top of something, it gets yanked out from under you.

Most people enter and exit this hyperbolic chamber somewhere between twelve and fifteen. I've never gotten out. My life has rarely come close to gelling. After living in more than a hundred homes, working close to a hundred jobs and making love to more than a hundred women, I'm still figuring out what I want to be when I grow up. I'm still on the ledge, waiting for wings.

Sometimes I have flying dreams so vivid that upon waking I feel the wind in my face, and take a moment to realize I can't fly.

My favorite variation is what I've come to think of as the kite: Standing on the ground near a big shade tree on the outskirts of a university campus, I aim my intention past the buildings into the sky. After one or two false starts I launch, twirling and spiraling till flight control kicks in and I work the astral winds like a sentient kite.

But like a kite, I can let out too much 'string', lose control and plummet until flight memory kicks in, as if from a former life. As it does, I'm thrilled to be able to speed up, slow down or change direction, but I remain wary of dark government forces who are after me for breaking the law of gravity—they don't want everyone knowing they can fly. So I wait for darkness before taking off on clandestine jaunts from roof to roof and shadow to shadow.

Around this part of the dream I usually spot this fantastically hot woman on the ground and can't resist swooping down to her. She asks how I can do this. I tell her flying's not so hard when you know how—anyone can, so long as they know they can. Until you know you can, you can't (which might be a kind of Sagittarian mantra).

I show her how to work the currents, which she tries, rising about an inch off the ground. We exchange this incredible look, like we've been waiting lifetimes for what's going to happen next. Just as we're about to fly off together, the dream usually ends....

In Santa Cruz in the early '90s I once had a much different flying dream, where I'm a giant, cyclopean, winged white whale, soaring majestically above a

sparkling city laid out in a crescent shape along the shores of an azure sea.

As I glide I'm aiming my huge frontal eye down, like a movie camera, slowly swiveling my head side to side, recording the landscape into the Akashic records (the Book of the Soul).

Not long after this dream I attended an exhibit at the Berkeley Art Museum, of drawings the famous educator, psychic and astrologer Rudolf Steiner doodled in the margins of his notes while giving public talks. I was stunned to spot a giant, cyclopean, winged whale next to a reference of Atlantis.

No synchronicity is incidental.

How did I know to dream this?

Is my life something that was once envisioned by a one-eyed whale?

Does déjà vu result from having previewed this incarnation ahead of time, then catching up to what you saw? Is that why some people you meet for the first time feel so familiar, and some experiences seem like you've gone through them before? Is the unzipped Sagittarian imagination the closest we get to wholescale reality? In the buzzing wilderness of medicine journeys, LSD excursions and ayahuasqueros, do we become more lucid than normal? What is normal, anyway?

Since the 1960s Revolution in Consciousness scared the daylights out of social controllers, who struck back with a vengeance, normalcy has become a Karmic Theatre presentation that might be called Pretending Reality Is So Much Less Than It Is. The ninth sign carries an antidote to this shrinkage because Sagittarius is the Great Unlimiter.[12]

---

[12] For more on Sixties backlash, see Operation Mockingbird, a CIA disinformation campaign begun in the 1950s and greatly expanded in the 1960s that recruited hundreds of operatives in US media to prevent racial integration and manipulate popular opinion to make it seem the powerful cultural transformations of the Sixties were caused by too many drugs. Unfortunately, it worked, as you can tell by many people's current opinion of what happened then.

The Unbound Glory
of Sagittarius:
The Art of Flying

H AVE YOU EVER EXPERIENCED A LIFE-CHANGING REVELA-
tion that exposes the Big Picture in such towering Technicolor
you can scarcely believe you used to languish in the gray half-
life of limited thinking below?

Zen Buddhists describe such awakenings as *satori*—implosions of
enlightenment—but they could also be called *centaur fuel* because it's
what Sagittarians run on.

With the possible exception of next-door neighbor Capricorn (sometimes featured as a seagoat rather than mountain goat), Saj is the only sign
depicted by a mythological creature. Rams, cows, twins, crabs and all the
rest inhabit the world we're accustomed to, but centaurs dwell beyond
the fields we know. As the zodiac's most mythical creature, Sagittarius
spends about half its time trying to prove it's real, the other half bridling
against *having* to be real.

When the centaur charges to the top of a hill, plucks an arrow from its
quiver, draws back the bow, aims at the sky and releases the shaft with so
much force it bursts into flame, then gallops after it, that's human nature
striving to catch up to its higher self. That's the urge buried in all humans—
but not so deeply buried in Sagittarians—to lift off the ground and fly.

Modern life is a stone-cold drag compared to what it could be. I know,
because I was adolescent in 1967, when the whole world went through
adolescence. Sagittarius is considered the sign of good fortune, and
with Saj Moon and Rising I consider myself one of the luckiest people

alive—to have been a teenager during the greatest party on Earth, which I wouldn't have missed for all the money in the world.

Collective consciousness opened wide enough then to receive a cosmic download that gave us a blueprint for a living future to replace the dead one being whipped up by the military-industrial complex, aided and abetted by corporate media.

Despite its superficialities and excesses—which were legion—the Love Revolution demonstrated the evolutionary surge that happens when millions of people choose love and freedom above conformity and constraint. The light that shone over the world then has kept me lit ever since, enabling me to ignite the light in others.

Even if you missed that party, you once were an adolescent on the verge of something indescribably beautiful. You once were an arrow yearning to fly.

I wonder about the strange fate of centaurs, who are more and less than equine, and more and less than human. A human unlike other humans and a horse unlike other horses seems a creature constantly in motion.

Cursed by the gods with eternal unrest for some ancient transgression, I imagine centaurs spurring themselves on in search of a breakthrough that can dispel the curse and set their species free. Though their genesis is cloaked in the mists of antiquity and, like many Greek and Roman myths, probably originated prior to the Greeks and Romans, one prominent tale pins their origin on a nasty trick of Zeus's.

To test a mortal king he suspected of lusting after his wife, Zeus concocted history's first sex-doll honey trap. To substantiate his suspicion, the mighty king of the gods transformed a cloud into an imitation Hera, whom the mortal king mistook for the real thing and had intercourse with.

I wonder if when Zeus watched the man-king get down with the decoy, he was reminded of all the delectable mortal women he'd knocked up, or if that inconvenient truth eluded even his omniscient vision.

Impregnated by the subterfuge, Cloud-Hera delivers a monstrous son with the head and torso of a man and lower body of a horse. For a long time I puzzled over why the faux Hera would birth such a creature, until I realized that the enormous size of a horse's penis was probably Zeus's ironic warning of what befalls mortals who lust after gods.

A king whose son was a monster would be shamed and cursed, as would his lineage, and lineage was sacrosanct to the Greeks. (Interestingly, though they don't feature in any tale I know of, female centaurs pop up here and there in classical Hellenic art, which causes one's imagination to wander....)

Unusually susceptible to wine, these horse-people were infamous for their out-of-control appetites and lusty carousing (there's that big dick again). A whole war was even named after them: The Centauromachy, begun when a herd of centaurs abducted their cousin's women during a wedding feast.

Despite their rapacious libido, one of their kind, Chiron, achieved great renown as a wisdom keeper and healer, to the extent that gods and mortals trained with him, including Asclepius, Greek god of healing, whose staff is the international symbol for medicine (often confused with Hermes's caduceus, which is twisted round with two snakes instead of one).

Like the mythical creature associated with them, Sagittarians tend to leap barriers and transgress boundaries. More than mortal, less than god, the centaur combines the primal instincts of a beast with the intellect of a human, and bow and arrows that suggest a touch of Olympian far-sightedness.

The prior sign, Scorpio, was so obsessed with latching onto primal truth that it generated a pressure Saj inherits the way a jack crammed in a box inherits the cranking of the handle. After the intense compression of Scorpio, there's scant chance of the centaur staying crammed in any box. Out of Scorpionic gravitas comes the flamboyance of the Archer; many Sagittarians wear normalcy like a loose-fitting garment about to shred at the slightest provocation. Like a teenager, Saj is strong on impulse, loaded with ambition, chock full of theory, but spotty on application and, especially when young, weak in follow-through.

Driven by impulses that could go anywhere or nowhere, learning to wrangle those that can be brought to Earth out of those best left in the clouds can be a long-term Sagittarian knockabout. Some signs are daunted by lack of enthusiasm or imagination; this one's challenged by an abundance.

Each sign is best understood as a journey rather than fixed state, but Saj is Journey itself: life as visionquest. The Archer is the constant traveler, who must develop a different set of skills than those of homebodies.[13]

We're all travelers. No one is indigenous to the physical plane because we originated in realms of spirit. Like centaurs, we're hybrid creatures, made of flesh and spirit, which clash and combine, then clash again, as human flesh fights physical limits, and human spirit strives to live up to its higher knowing.

To make the most of the hybrid state is to move through life like an honored guest moving through somebody else's realm, where nothing is permanently yours but borrowed. Treading gingerly, as you would in some exotic land where they do things much differently than in your home country, is an excellent way to gain the traveler's blessing.

Though Sagittarians are built for motion (think of those massive horse thighs), a major rite of passage occurs when they evolve ways to travel while standing still. Here's a glimpse from one who did:

...To see a World in a Grain of Sand
And a Heaven in a Wild Flower
Hold Infinity in the palm of your hand
And Eternity in an hour...

from *Auguries of Innocence* by William Blake (18th-century Sagittarian visionary, poet and artist).

---

[13] The zodiac becomes much more dynamic and interactive when you think of each sign as a journey rather than fixed state. As a Libra I shouldn't be expected to know everything there is to know about love, but to commit to a journey toward finding out everything I can about that profound subject. If I pay attention I can make the most of that ride and call it a life. Someone setting out to master their zodiacal qualities has got to put their foot in it over and over to get anywhere.

Though he was born in the middle of the 1700s, Blake's cosmic visions enjoyed a heyday two hundred years later in the 1960s. With the geography of nations heavily mapped then, the geography of the mind became the hot new real estate. Blake was recruited as one of the cosmic Sherpas from the past who could guide us to the future with transcendent imagery that presided over the rollicking heights and vertiginous plunges of many mushroom journeys and mescaline trips.

Art speaks to the visionary capacity of this sign, because with no lids on their imaginations, history's artists have advanced human consciousness more than have presidents and kings. The most sublime art erects signposts pointing to a world within the world.

A heady cocktail of egoic bluster, youthful escapism, fiery libido and optimistic vision is the constitutional chemistry of this sign. To determine where that's going requires giving Saj flights of fancy the benefit of the doubt that they may prove to be more than hot air. They frequently do, but not always, because rather than waiting for everything to line up before leaping, centaurs tend to leap first. Many leaps fall flat, but fear of failure is unlikely to flatten this sign as much as never having tried.

Known for big hearts and restless minds, Sagittarians tend to be gregarious and expansive (as you might expect from the king of the gods) rather than petty and picayune. Such largesse is well-suited for grand dreaming but can strand the sign in seductive theoretical flights that overlook important details needed to make those dreams real.

Astrological tradition views Sagittarians as the mouthpiece of the gods, and one rarely knows what might emerge from their mouths. Often they themselves don't know, due to their penchant for speaking before they think, and firing words like arrows. Some strike the target and some strike unintended targets, but in its pressing need to get things moving, Saj rarely bogs down worrying about bruised feelings, which centaurs typically shrug off then gallop on. Because they often think with their mouths, it can surprise them as much as anyone when provocative assertions they dash off in passing turn out true.

Blake espoused progressive ideas far beyond the thinking of his time (or any time), protesting the horrors of slavery and challenging the rule of religion, but this provocative visionary went largely unrecognized in his day. Of the relatively few who were aware of him, many thought he was mad due to his firebranding iconoclasm and anti-Church ravings. Though he lived to a ripe old age, such incendiary art costs some artists not only their reputations but their lives.

Even today artists languish in prison in places where the rich and powerful fear the radical forces their art might unleash. If you gallop around with a quiver of arrows, you're bound to rattle cages and burn bridges. Such missiles, though, can conflagrate the low ceiling of collective thought and inspire human consciousness to aim higher.

Saj is the holy fool, daring the universe to meet it in fields of splendor, as became evident to the young lass who stumbled upon Blake as an old man in the fresh air, painting at an easel the way he loved to paint near the end of his life—stark naked—and they became fast friends. Blake's *plein air au naturel* didn't seem the dotage of an old codger's declining years so much as consistent with his lifelong devotion to the transcendental; he died singing of the things he saw in heaven.

Archers are on fire to activate, optimize, amplify, build, stretch, link ideas, extend theories and discover trends, and so tend to be in a state of perpetual overwhelm and probably wouldn't have it any other way. If some glittering possibility comes flashing down the pike, they want in, otherwise they're likely to get bored and bolt. Where evolutionary options arise you'll find centaurs ready to leap, and where thought becomes stunted you'll find them chafing at the bit.

Sagittarius is the zodiac's *more;* whatever there is, there's always *more.*

Blake encapsulated *more*-ness when he quipped, "If the fool would persist in his folly he would become wise." It's not enough, if you cut a chink in the wall of restrictive thought, to peer through half-heartedly while remaining safe on this side. But if, like a holy fool, you persist in digging open the chink, you might *break on through to the other side,* as Sagittarian Jim Morrison of the Doors urged us to do.

Morrison could be the poster boy for Sagittarian *more* because he never seemed to get enough, and his hunger appeared equal parts intellectual and libidinous, typifying the centaur's spicy mix of carnality and consciousness. In the Sixties many Boomers got our first reference to shamanism from his book of poetry. You can feel the following arrow strike as sharply now as when he first twanged it from his bow:

> The most important kind of freedom is to be what you really are. You trade in your reality for a role... You give up your ability to feel, and in exchange, put on a mask.

In Morrison, the urge for self-destruction seemed to vie with a holy mission to save the human race from itself. True to the incendiary spirit of the times, he constellated the Dionysian side of radical freedom, which makes me wonder: Once Sagittarius breaks on through, where does she go? After you hold infinity in the palm of your hand, what do you do with it?

Probably the most optimistic sign and (along with Aries and Gemini) one of the most restless, Saj is inclined to keep bouncing off the last dream toward the next, an operating strategy that (especially when young) hits the jackpot less frequently than goes broke. Is the Archer getting seduced by a cloud or making love to something real? Are you courting freedom or disaster?

A key to wrangling Sagittarian dreams is to lavish care on the small steps needed to concretize the big visions. Instead of dashing off after the next and next, slowing down to tend to what's already begun can be a key turning point for such a high-spirited sign. Like tossing a halter over a runaway centaur, it can take years of getting bucked off before Saj sits firmly in the saddle.

Each sign picks up the legacy of the previous and transforms it for the subsequent. Of all transitions from one sign to the next, none is as dramatic as the immense release from Scorpio to Saj. After being cooped up in scorpion bone yards, who could blame Archers for firing arrows willy-nilly and galloping after them? Scorpio is a mighty bow whose drawstring is pulled back until the wood is about to burst; Saj is the release of the arrow.

The locus between the real and imaginary is Sagittarian proving grounds, with some boundaries getting transgressed that probably shouldn't, and others remaining in place that might be better not. The ninth sign's tendency to push boundaries can be understood in light of its proximity not just to nearby signs, but to the center of our galaxy, which it has a unique relationship with.

When we look at the Milky Way in the night sky, the stellar population in that part of the heavens coalesces into the famous river of stars that appears once you get far enough from city lights. That river is due to Earth's view seat on the galaxy.

To visualize this, imagine the relatively flat plane of our galaxy as a spiral of glitter, embedded in a thick but transparent dinner plate slowly spinning on a dining room table. Earth is about two-thirds of the way from the center of the plate towards its outer rim.

When you look at Sagittarius from Earth, you're looking from the general vicinity of the rim toward the hub. Because you're viewing the galaxy edge-on into the thick of it, you're gazing through hundreds of billions more stars than if you were looking toward the rim, or if you were gazing out of the galactic plane, for example, toward the floor or ceiling of the dining room. The extra stars you're peering through merge into the glittering band we call the Milky Way.

Sagittarius is the only astrological constellation that points us toward galactic center, but the center of our galaxy is visually blocked from us by the Great Rift—ginormous cosmic dust clouds that permanently obstruct the view. Similarly, Sagittarian leaps of thought are often based on something harder to see than to sense.

As brightly shining as Sagittarian intellects tend to be, this sign's most unique contribution to the circle of twelve has less to do with its logic than with its fuller body of senses, especially those off the radar of what we usually think of as senses.

In ancient Greece, Aristotle said there are five senses, and that's what everyone's been saying since. A hundred years ago Rudolf Steiner said, *Why?*

Conventions like the five-sense model rule world thought. They dominate our paradigms. Elementary school teachers worship them. Science books parrot them. People take them for granted till some troublemaker comes along to upend the apple cart. Steiner identified twelve senses he linked with the twelve signs of the zodiac, and, since the matter is somewhat subjective, who's to say he's wrong? Perhaps there are even more.

The five-sense model fails to account for telepathic communication (happens to me all the time), outrageous synchronicities (I've had a few), and other documented phenomena, such as dreaming things before they happen, warnings from dead relatives that come true, women who have spontaneous orgasms the moment their lover dies in some other part of the world, and insects and other animals with abilities far beyond those of you and me. If you travelled the world to sit at people's kitchen tables asking if they've experienced anything inexplicable by the old model, you'd be able to fill many books with their replies.

I see Sagittarius as best friends dropping acid on a drive through the galaxy, where the next bend of the spiral could strip off the outer casing of the universe or reconstruct your DNA. Best friends is close enough for travel buddies, yet not as karmic as lovers, lending grace to the excursion. If you keep your senses sharp, oil changed and windshield clear, the boundaries between the ordinary and miraculous may become much thinner than you think. In high school I crossed such a boundary when hitchhiking to Boston, 150 miles away from my hometown of Stratford, Connecticut.

I'd been regularly thumbing that route to visit my college lover Sandra. But I'd skipped school so many times to see her I'd gotten in hot water with my parents and teachers, so when Sandra phoned to ask if I wanted to go to a sold-out Johnny Winter concert scheduled for two weeks later at the Boston Garden, which her friend had gotten us tickets for, I said I'd love to but had to pass.

When the day of the concert came, though, as Johnny's lightning-streaked blues-rock played in the back of my brain I couldn't take it any longer, so I rushed to my school's art wing, made a Boston sign, marched off the grounds, and raised my thumb at the entrance to I-95.

My first ride dropped me off one exit later, where another took me a few more exits.

The green Pontiac that pulled over for my third ride in the suburbs of New Haven had three people in it. I slid in back, made greetings all around, and asked the driver, "Where ya goin'?"

She said, "Boston—we're going to a concert."

"Which one?"

"Just the greatest guitarist on Earth—Johnny Winter."

"*Oh wow!* You wouldn't happen to have an extra ticket? My girlfriend's going and I'd love to join her, but it's sold out."

The driver shrugged. Indicating the guy next to her, she said, "His friend in the city has the tickets. She might have an extra. You can check with her when we get there."

Two hours later we pulled up to college dorms in downtown Boston. I asked the girl if she had an extra ticket. She said, "Huh. Funny you ask— matter of fact, I do, because my friend's boyfriend was gonna come—*but decided not to.*"

I got goose bumps, as this person turned out to be Sandra's friend. Similar to the man who had an appointment in Samarra (but with a much happier ending), I'd managed to buy my own ticket![14]

On the Connecticut Turnpike, where thousands of vehicles roar by every hour, how did the first and second cars manage to deposit me at the perfect place to get picked up by the third? How did I happen to paint my sign and leave my school at just that moment? What were the people in the Pontiac doing beforehand that led them to depart

---

[14] Appointment in Samarra: One morning a Baghdad merchant sent his brother to market for provisions. Very soon the brother came back empty-handed, trembling, and said, "I was jostled by a woman in the marketplace, and when I turned I saw it was Death. She made a threatening gesture and I ran here straightaway. Brother—you must lend me your horse, and I will ride away to avoid my fate. I will ride to Samarra where Death cannot find me." The merchant immediately lent his brother the horse, and the brother rode fast as he could. Then the merchant went to market, saw Death in the crowd, and asked her, "Why did you make a threatening gesture at my brother?" "Eh? Oh, that," death replied, raising one finger. "That was not a threatening gesture—it was only a start of surprise. I was astonished to see him this morning in Baghdad, for I had an appointment with him tonight in Samarra."

precisely when they did? Statisticians could have a field day calculating the odds against this.

The hitchhiking synchronicity was my initial clue that some larger design is at work in what I'd considered a random or capricious universe, a design I might've missed had I stayed in my classroom.

By leaping into the greater classroom of the moment (courtesy of Saj Moon and Rising)—which in this case meant skipping school and stepping into the apparently not-so-random random river of traffic—I seem to have drawn a thread of pattern into weave that would've otherwise remained loose. Since then I've stumbled into synchronicities even more amazing, which has shored up my sense of a grand design.

Sagittarius is the force of change that propels you out of your familiar setting, like a Hobbit sprung from the Shire. It's that moment you and your friends lean forward in a theater as the house lights dim and your favorite band takes the stage.

The Saj in us longs to gather in the mystic village known by different names in different cultures: *Shambhala. El Dorado. Shangri-La. Brigadoon. Tanelorn. Rivendell,* where wise and beautiful women, mighty heroes and wandering troubadours share food and talk deep into the night. I can think of few more glorious visions, and suspect I'm not alone in that.[15]

Since the 1970s I've entered Tanelorn many times when the locale I lived in became a flashpoint for a small circle of souls who gathered in the hills and cafés, ate magic mushrooms and played music all night under the stars. Few of my experiences compare with the exquisite camaraderie of those moments, which I've done my best to sustain, though they always seem to vanish when some cosmic clock runs out and the mystic village reverts to Monday morning traffic.

Regarding centaurs, I ponder whether the horse symbolizes our lower nature and the human represents our higher, or vice versa. Horses are

---

[15] Probably the least well-known of these idyllic realms, Tanelorn is the eternal constant, the ever-recurring city in Michael Moorcock's reincarnational Eternal Hero fantasy trilogies, where fifteen planes of existence intersect, and temporary respite at the feasting table can be found from the insane Gods of Chaos and Law.

known for great intelligence, enormous strength and telepathic bonds with their humans. Humans are known for fantastic ingenuity and self-destruction.

When human consciousness is matched against other animals, old-school behavioral scientists insist we're superior. They love to proclaim our consciousness more advanced, but there's evidence to the contrary. (Octopuses, in fact, may have us beat.[16]) Cutting-edge researchers have begun to recognize human consciousness as simply one kind, not necessarily higher than animals, mostly just *different* than, and in some respects, lower.[17]

The old dope on this, such as we're the only animal who feels feelings, uses tools and recognizes afterlife, has been debunked, by otters who use rocks to crack mussel shells, and elephants who not only return to pachyderm graveyards on annual migrations, but walk directly to the skull of their deceased mate, look down and cry tears.[18]

Like the centaur, humanity is a mutt, made of stars and clay. That sounds like poetic exaggeration but is more scientifically accurate than you may think. The iron in your blood came from white dwarf stars that released heavy metals on galactic winds, which got captured by Earth, so you're literally made of stars. Nitrogen, the vital prerequisite for life, apparently was dropped off from deep space to newborn Earth by the frozen snowballs we call comets, so you're made of comets.

Stars and comets, part terrestrial, part extraterrestrial, human aspiration strives to rise out of the mud of limited thinking. Claiming a brief moment of glory, we fire arrows of ambition at the sky then, when our time is up, like spent arrows clatter back to the ground.

---

[16] See the recent tender and fascinating exploration of animal consciousness in Sy Montgomery's *The Soul of an Octopus.*

[17] For more on this, check the warmhearted classic memoir on human-to-animal telepathy, *Kinship with All Life,* by J. Allen Boone.

[18] As described in the eye-opening, well-researched book *When Elephants Weep,* by Masson and McCarthy.

Sagittarius is the dreamer dreaming of soaring beyond history's Great Rift into a supernal dimension that, like the center of our galaxy, remains harder to see than it is to sense.

Many of us dream of a bright future for our species. Many dwell in the outskirts of a mystic village. In some finer realm, perhaps, we're already there, you and I, raising goblets under cascading blossoms of purple wisteria, constructing houses of moon and starlight. But in the coarser physical dimension we wake up in each morning we just can't seem to get our shit together.

Sagittarians thrive on the next big thing, and adore festivals like Oregon Country Fair or Burning Man, where instead of getting blotto for no reason, the celebration is one of love and art-magic rocketing up inspirational flights of consciousness.

But after the festival, regularity reasserts itself. After every *satori,* Saj has to do the dishes and dump the trash. Like Neanderthals bumping into the base of a towering plateau, human beings scramble out of a limiting stage of awareness onto the higher ground of a new vista that we ecstatically jump up and down on, until the new becomes old and we search for a *new* new.

Inspiration and expansion are the birthrights of those born under the Sign of the Archer, who tend to be folks that others are drawn to. Human nature *wants* to follow a beautiful dream to some iteration of El Dorado, where the weary soul can find respite and the sumptuous feast glows long into the night.

Higher consciousness feeds the mind like food feeds the body, and many Sagittarians love to feed both. The magnanimity of this sign can produce some of the zodiac's freest forms of giving. Perhaps more than any other sign, Saj instinctively knows life is good, and for it to be lived to the last drop needs to be shared.

At best, Sagittarius fosters a warm spirit of camaraderie, eager to spread the great good news of being. At worst, Saj is the repetitious distortion that occurs when sensory appetites turn destructive, and more is never enough.

Like a horny high school girl sneaking out of her bedroom window to party, Saj is the surge of the spirit to break external restriction. The rising arc of the arrow's flight lifts us toward heights of glory, like Sagittarian Jimi Hendrix lighting his guitar on fire and combusting previous concepts of music, while its sinking arc brings us down to earth when the party's over. Late at night, as her legs wobble and eyesight dims, the schoolgirl still has to make her way to bed. And after Jimi lights up his Stratocaster, he needs to buy a new one.

As high as we fly on wings of revelation, gravity eventually thumps us back to the here-and-now. As stuck as we get in limiting thought, some cosmic thrust in our DNA rockets us back to our starry origins—and in 1953 when he discovered DNA, Francis Crick was soaring on LSD.

The DNA double helix is an appropriate symbol for the dual spiraling action of this sign. Like a psychedelic barber-shop pole, Sagittarius spirals our attention up toward the infinite, down to the here-and-now, and round and round the material plane. The constant motion of that red stripe, when turned to a multicolor mescaline wash, can produce vertigo unless the cycles are trimmed, so that hurtling toward the next destination becomes less escapist, and grounding back into daily rhythms becomes less of a train wreck.

To run free with your mates, slake your thirst at a feast of the senses, leap from revelation to revelation, and not get dopey-drunk but gloriously sober, is a gorgeous Sagittarian dream.

The Saj nightmare is when your daily routine strays so far from the life you were born to live that it fences you in, while the centaur in you kicks the beams of a burning barn to get out.

Most of us yearn to be more than we used to be. At sixty-eight I haven't outgrown that yearning any more than I had at sixteen. In fact, it may be stronger.

Whether or not their arrows strike target, we need Archers to lift our vision and extend our reach. A world without Sagittarians would be a dreary place. The obsession of Scorpio and intensity of Capricorn would blow up the home stretch of the zodiac if it weren't for the *sangfroid* of the ninth sign.

When a sign is this hooked on what *can* be, it sometimes misses the deeper cut of what *is*. Much of life will fail to whet Sagittarian appetites. Many experiences will bore them to death. Many ideas will leave them flat. Most centaurs will gallop down more dead-ends than roads to Shambhala. It can exhaust Saj-watchers to keep track. But for sheer indefatigable enthusiasm, no sign is greater. None has more resilience. No matter how many times this sign gets knocked down, it bounces back stronger.

I wonder if some imp ambushes Sagittarius's well-laid plans to give it the fun of reinventing itself. The sign's secret superpower is the fountain of youth of discovering a new skill or talent throughout life, especially late in the game. If a dollop of immaturity and bucket of risk is the price to pay for keeping such dreams alive, it's a trifling fee.

I believe the *more* that Sagittarius hungers for may be achieved by awakening powers of perception that normally lie dormant. Without going anywhere you can fly the Milky Way when your senses open.

One spring night in 1996, in Santa Cruz, where I was living, I attended Ellias Lonsdale's class on the sign of Cancer, which happened to be my father's sign. I'd said a final goodbye to Dad two days earlier in a V.A. hospital in St. Petersburg, Florida, where he lay dying of Waldenstrom's lymphoma, and had left him in the capable hands of my mother.

As class ended, I started trembling but didn't know why, and asked my friends Rochelle and Alissa if they'd walk me out because something strange was happening to me. I crawled into the back seat of my vintage Volvo, and they climbed in, sandwiching me. For two hours, while they held onto me, my body shook and spasmed, then became completely still.

The next morning my mom called from Florida and said, "Your father died last night after two hours of spasms," which turned out to be the same two hours.

No synchronicity is incidental. How is it that my conscious awareness didn't know what was happening three thousand miles away, but some other part of me did? Why does it require something as drastic as dying to awaken such faculties?

I believe Dad's spirit recruited me as a kind of midwife to divert the pain of his passing and free him to move on. I'll be forever grateful I was able to do that for him, even though I didn't know what I was doing. But maybe he did. He may also have boosted me by pouring his final life force into my body, since he wasn't going to need it anymore. Even now sometimes I believe I can feel him stirring in me, when life piles up and I need a boost.

Of all the awesome synchronicities, wild adventures and provocative revelations Sagittarius experiences, the most wonderful may be that it doesn't know what it's doing. Sometimes being present is more crucial than being in the know, and when you're too much in the know you may fail to be present.

It's natural for Saj to want to get in on the next big thing, but some deeper force than social ambition drives the soul of this sign. Like the mysterious link that drew me into my father's passing, and in keeping with Blake's adage that to go deeper into your folly can lead to wisdom, the innocence of the zodiac's biggest Fool may end up going where its logic fears to tread.

Could the everyday state of an unconditioned human being be the *more* the Sagittarian part of us is after? Could it be that to activate not just the five senses we know about, but *all* our senses, would catapult us beyond history's Great Rift?

To be magical is the natural Sagittarian default, and the nature of us all. To be real and magical is what we have to learn. Realness at the expense of magic creates a dull world. Magic at the expense of realness can be ungrounding and escapist. Balancing the two is a grand adventure for this sign.

Saj is so naturally attuned to the visionary side of things, it's easy for it to confuse the ideal with the real. It's tempting to relate to the expanded future state of someone or something rather than get bogged down by the drag of its current condition.

When I began writing this book, I sent a chapter for possible serialization to a prestigious astrology magazine that has published my material before, and they turned me down flat with a clipped, cutting and almost rude dismissal.

Now that I look back upon the state the chapter was in then, I realize that my Saj Moon and Rising had already leaped into a glorious future version of the book, which I couldn't expect an editor to grok. That version is only now being born after four years of labor. If I'd been a magazine editor four years ago (as I was in the 1980s) I might've also turned me down (though I would've done so with more grace).

My Saj tendency to leap before I look often merges with my Libran idealism and Scorpionic obsessiveness to produce a relationship effect I haven't heard others mention. Especially when younger, but sometimes even now, whenever I saw a woman I was drawn to (which was several times a week or sometimes several times a day), I rocketed to the future stage of our connection, a state so visceral I could taste and smell it. That future gripped me by the short hairs in a way that could be very disconcerting in light of our current connection—which was often no connection at all.

Similar leaps occurred when I met potential music partners and was flung into the music we were going to make. Once in a blue moon, if I happened to meet a woman I was attracted to who was also a musician, I got helplessly lost, drowning in futures.

A few of those leaps landed on solid ground, and we *did* get to be friends, lovers or music partners. The overwhelming majority dissipated, though some of those visions still linger.

Sagittarius longs to be free but must outgrow the adolescent understanding of the word, which is freedom *from,* such as 'When I get rid of (fill in the blank: my clueless mother, my dickhead boyfriend, my dead-end job, my clunky body), I'll finally be free....' But that sort of freedom often turns out to be a carrot on the stick attached to the head of a donkey, which, if you ever catch up to it, gets replaced by the next carrot and the next.

The richest treasures of the Sagittarian visionquest arise when we gain a freedom more intrinsic than relative, less to do with getting *out* of anything, and more to do with getting *in* to the full-spectrum awareness few of us get to without impending catastrophes or sacred medicines.

When you become ultra-present rather than ultra-checked-out (as many people seem to be these days), there's no need to go anywhere because there's nowhere else to go. Life becomes a palette you can paint with rather than roulette wheel you're at the random effect of. Like during a medicine journey, your participation in the multidimensional crossweave becomes less obscure and more illuminated.

If we emerge beyond confining corrals such as the five-sense model as a matter of course rather than only during ecstatic festivals, medicine journeys or when someone is dying, the *more* we seek may arrive right where we stand.

Picking up the torch of the bright ones who found worlds in grains of sand and heavens in wild flowers, perhaps we wouldn't have to die to sing of the things in heaven, but could sing of them while still alive. Perhaps we wouldn't need LSD to break on through to the other side, just our enhanced perception.

Here's to the Sagittarian bards and minstrels, innovative thinkers, wild gamblers and holy fools, who show us who we are and who we might be. May the dream of sharing rich camaraderie in a real live Rivendell lift the curse off the centaur, and restore the living goddess among us rather than the one made of clouds.

SAGITTARIUS DRAGONHEAD/GEMINI DRAGONTAIL

From the local view to the big picture

With Gemini behind you and Sagittarius ahead, you're departing from the local view and heading toward the big picture. That doesn't mean ignoring what's in your immediate vicinity, just not getting so wrapped up in the scenery that you lose track of the map. Throughout your reincarnational journey you shapeshifted through so many variations on the theme of being human that you don't need to keep adding more and more so much as fire up ideas big enough to stretch your imagination and do justice to the full scope of your ride. You'll never understand half of what the gods are telling you, but don't let the fact you're a cosmic fool keep you from galloping your centaur high into the eyries of dragons. Human foolery appears like emergency flares from that perch, because the more we stumble around down here, the more we draw the attention of celestial forces that need us to show them where to send their roadside assistance. Along with many other skills, you're a mouthpiece through which the gods sometimes speak, which doesn't mean you always have to know what you're doing, just that your willingness to serve goes a long way.

From the big picture to the local view

SAGITTARIUS DRAGONTAIL/GEMINI DRAGONHEAD

With Sagittarius behind you and Gemini ahead, you're departing from the big picture and heading toward the local view. Often the reverse path is more appealing, because it's less messy. Like strong lysergic acid, your mind's so compelling it's easy to trip out and get lost there, so it's up to your friends and your body (and your friends' bodies) to reach in and pluck you out. You're journeying from exotic locales to the air you breathe and the ground you walk on, zooming in from generalities to specifics. After hobnobbing in past-life halls of power, you're after the extraordinariness of the ordinary, which admits you to a fantastic realm that may look normal but becomes a multidimensional playground when you get inside it. Because the number of things you want to do will always dwarf the amount you're getting done, it's all about opening your heart.

CHAPTER TEN

Beware Capricorns whose reach no longer exceeds their grasp, because they'll lose their magic if they stop challenging themselves.

To be human is to be fallible. To be human is to have a higher awareness difficult to access. To be human is to trip over your own two feet.

To be a goat is to hunger. To be a goat is to play. To be a goat is to climb.

To be Capricorn is to search for what's real, what's essential, what endures, and what counts.

Soul-Wrestling on the Transcendental Highway: The Capricorn Art of Making Everything Count

C APRICORN IS THE YEARNING FOR MASTERY. IT'S THE COM-
mitment to use everything and waste nothing on the way to
master that portion of life your soul is steering you toward, and
the caution that without self-mastery, no worldly success will take you
where you need to go.

Though astrology texts sometimes depict this sign as a mountain
goat, its ancient depiction was of a seagoat, who combines the playful, stubborn, libidinous, high-climbing aspirations of a goat with the
deep-diving mystery of a mermaid.

By the laws of physics it'd be impossible to get these two creatures
into one, since the goat would drown in water and the mermaid would
asphyxiate in air. This suggests practical thinking alone won't take
Capricorn where it wants to go without the addition of magical thinking.

When linked to the upper body of a goat, the finned tail of the seagoat
evokes the soul-wrestling part of the Capricorn journey: To earn a higher
stage of consciousness you first have to do justice to the stage you're at, and
learn its lessons. You can only climb as far *up* as you're willing to delve *down*.
You can only authentically ascend the mountain of success insofar as you're
willing to dive into the submerged contents of your psyche and clean your
inner mess. If you transcend without fully incarnating, it'll be premature.
You'll end up having to go back later to deal with unfinished business.

By this advanced stage of the zodiac, the only kind of mastery
Capricorn's going to settle for is the real deal. To gain that, you don't

need to avoid mistakes so much as make every mistake in the book and learn from it.

For some reason I haven't been able to figure out, this sign seems to have more variations than any other, from highly sexed to chastely celibate, passionately on fire to quietly humdrum, politically radical to unbudgingly conservative. I've known Caps more frivolous than the most frivolous Gemini and more tightly wound than the most tightly wound Cancer, more out on the edge than the wildest Aquarian, and more calm than the most placid Taurus.

Seagoats can't gain the mastery they seek by trimming their extremes. Only by pushing the spectrum can they learn what they're made of. That means stress-testing their hunches and theories until their experiential learning catches at least halfway up to their dreams, an epic journey for this epic sign, rather than a quick fix.

Capricorns (along with Aquarians) are the latest bloomers in the zodiac. Other signs, with roads less steep, may take less time to get where they're going, but Capricorn can't climb to the top of its mountain without corkscrews, detours and double-backs, and can't delve to its depths without overcoming monsters of the deep.

In some illustrations of seagoats, such as the Tropic of Capricorn latitudes on ancient maps, their mer-tail winds around so much that, if unrolled, would measure three or four times the length of the goat part. This suggests that in your urgency for material gain, you should be even more urgent to clean your karma.

The Tao states:

> Nothing is weaker than water,
> But when it attacks something hard
> Or resistant, then nothing withstands it,
> And nothing will alter its way.

> Everyone knows this, that weakness prevails
> Over strength and that gentleness conquers
> The adamant hindrance of men, but that
> Nobody demonstrates how it is so.

Because of this the wise man says
That only one who bears the nation's shame
Is fit to be its hallowed lord;
That only one who takes upon himself
The evils of the world may be its king.

This is paradox.

As the zodiac winds down to its last three signs, Capricorn's position, following Virgo, Libra, Scorpio and Saj, gives it much to live up to, because each of these builds upon the passion of the previous, which is why I call the stretch from Virgo to Cap *The Passion Corridor*. By the time we reach the seagoat, pressure's on to raise human awareness to its highest before pitching the journey into the wild curve of the last two signs.

From thrifty Virgo, Capricorn inherits passion for self-reliance. From Libra, it receives passion for union. From Scorpio, Capricorn inherits the passion to live from the soul. And from fiery next-door neighbor Saj, Cap inherits the passion to exceed limits.

Combining these drives into one helluva horny, high-climbing, deep-diving seagoat increases the stakes for the tenth sign, whose life art is best understood as a rich and demanding karma-yoga: Between the constricting passageways of your inner turmoil and brilliant landscape of your optimal future lies the ultimate stretch, which pits your dreams against your fears to stretch your selfhood into shape.

Climbing the mountain of higher consciousness requires the pace of a marathon instead of a sprint, because there are many drives and counter-drives within a single human being. One part of you is in love with something another part can't stand. One part of you is clear as a bell, another discombobulated as a train wreck. The more you dig, the more you'll wrestle with the Taoist paradox mentioned above.

Which leads to the blessing of karma.

Karma isn't usually seen as a blessing, due to popular misconception of what it's all about. Most people think karma is payback for past wrongs, or reward for past rights, but neither of these is its main purpose. The main purpose of karma is to invite your full presence and participation in life, by challenging you to awaken in the places you've been asleep, and to show up in the places you've been absent.

Each of us has vacant lots and unoccupied channels, which are empty classrooms where we fail to engage the wholeness of our being and avoid learning the lessons our soul signed up for. As a member of the species taking the longest time of any on the planet to grow up, karma is the universe's way of getting your attention.

If you've been dissatisfied, dysfunctional or incomplete with sex; if you've been dissatisfied, dysfunctional or incomplete with money; if you've been dissatisfied, dysfunctional or incomplete with creative expression, health, self-love or family, your karma will keep delivering reruns in these areas, not as punishment, but as opportunities to awaken. To grasp the opportunity requires wrestling with the paradoxical recognition that the rerun of the pattern provides your best chance to get beyond it.

Rather than your worst enemy, karma is your best friend and the most loyal lover you'll ever find, the one that'll never give up on you. Regardless of how many times you fail to get its message, your karma will never say, 'Um, I asked you to wake up in 15th-century Romania and you didn't. I asked you to wake up in 19th-century Chicago, and you didn't. I asked you to wake up 99 times in your current life, and you didn't, so I'm done asking.'

No.

Your karma will say, 'I asked you to wake up 99 times and you didn't, so I'm asking a hundredth.'

The way karma asks you to awaken is by delivering a current variation on your unresolved issues, which provides the best opportunity for you to do something new with them.

When your karma comes back and instead of caving in you awaken to the dream hidden in the nightmare, you begin to turn it around.

Such psychic judo requires the playfulness of a goat and implacability of a Buddha, because it's hard to awaken from dysfunction until it reconstitutes, but once it reconstitutes it's hard not to fall for it again. Try as you might to get to the dragon's head, you keep getting whacked by its tail.

The perceptual judo flip from karma to grace begins once you realize the return of the pattern is more opportunity than calamity, because until it returns one more time—hopefully, not a *lot* more times—you can't gain purchase on it. You lack leverage. It hangs like a blob of clay that hasn't landed on the potter's wheel. It hovers on the edge of your awareness, haunting your new starts with the memory of how earlier forays in those directions didn't pan out. It can be very hard to think of yourself as lucky in love when love is crumbling around you once more, but that's the very moment you have to find something new inside of something old to turn the pattern around.

Our missing pieces invite our fuller arrival, and we all have missing pieces. No human is perfect. The greatest Capricorn irony is that the more you gain awareness, the more you realize how unaware you are! They neglect to tell you this in spiritual circles, often implying that once you gain enlightenment everything will go your way, as if the purpose of enlightenment is to make your ego fantasies come true. In my experience it's the opposite: You can tell you're on the road to enlightenment when everything around you falls apart because it was based largely on your partially awakened half-life.

In the previous stage, far-ranging Sagittarius fired flaming arrows beyond limited thinking, which expanded the scope of what's possible. For tough-minded Capricorn it's not enough to glimpse that land but to move in and inhabit it, which means digging out whatever's in the way, and persevering, because that dig may have several stages and take longer than you think.

To dwell so close to glory, to know you're capable of so much more than you've delivered, to be tantalized by the distant peak of your magnificent aspirations while crashing into your magnificent failures, are the proving grounds of this highly instinctual, extremely wily and enormously capable sign.

The ultimate karma-yoga stretch is the ability to recognize everything that happens as an invitation to awaken. Especially the most challenging things, because the places we're most blind are where we can gain the most vision. The places we're most ignorant are where we can gain the most understanding. And the places we're most stuck are where we're capable of the greatest freedom, but you really have to work that evolutionary ground over and over like a karmic bulldozer to get to the other side.

When everything that happens is seen as an invitation to awaken—though, admittedly, in extreme predicaments this can be very hard to do—your worst plights become wake-up calls to catalyze your greatest growth and transformation.

The great revelation of the seagoat is nothing lasts, but everything has meaning. Nothing stays the same, but everything counts. Nothing is useless, and all things have something to say—once you learn to listen.

The Capricorn blessing unfolds when you take up life as a phenomenal journey you're absolutely invested in and completely free of. One without the other is lopsided, because if you increase investment without increasing non-attachment, you'll burn out. And if you increase non-attachment without increasing investment, you'll fade away.

The balance of both can only be gained by the right use of power, something rare in any time, but especially rare in our time, with few role models of impeccable leadership, and a trash-talk-tarot-deck-full of front-page-supermarket-tabloid personalities vying to become the celebrity flavor of the month.

In ancient courts a skull was kept on the throne, grim reminder that no matter how much power a monarch gained, stronger forces would have final say. The grinning specter of self-destruction was never far from the high-and-mighty airs of kings.

Though I'm Libra, Capricorn holds the key to my birth chart, and is my Dragonhead, the place I'm trying to get to. You could say my life is in the key of Capricorn, which means the insights I offer in this chapter are probably the ones I worked hardest to gain.

One of my greatest insights came on a spring morning in 1988 in La Honda, the little mountain town in northern California where twenty-five years earlier LSD was first used recreationally by Ken Kesey and the Grateful Dead, and where I rented a small studio apartment with a tiny balcony overhanging a stream.

The studio was austere, modern, white and chrome—not my style, but it had a pristine feeling that compelled me to spend long hours studying metaphysics. I called it my Monk's Studio, because months earlier I'd split with my girlfriend in the city, after which I spent many hours alone.

I'd recently created Soul Level Astrology and begun making a name for myself, offering talks, classes and readings in the Bay Area, which boasted countless astrologers, and where launching my career was slow going for a thirty-three-year-old wannabe wizard, who'd lost more homes, jobs and girlfriends than most people ever find.

I'd worked odd jobs since high school, when I'd gotten fired from driving a drugstore delivery car, the first of many jobs I lost due to my inability to stifle my radical spirit and toe the corporate line. In recent years I'd been kicking around the comic book industry but hadn't gotten far with my writing, and had gotten sidetracked to the business end, in editing and promotion.

The more I strove to believe in a bright and lucrative future for myself, the more I remembered times in my childhood when my father came into my room with a heavy sense of resignation, confiding, "The landlord's going to sell and we can't afford to buy, so we'll have to move again."

Instead of going *toward* it seemed we were always going *away from*. As the new kid on the block, I kept having to let go and move on. And here, in the Santa Cruz Mountains, after decades of letting go and starting over, I was letting go and starting over. Now that I'd hung out my first professional shingle I had high hopes of my brand-new astrology career taking me to a financial solvency neither I nor my father had gotten to.

To advance my intuitive skills and assist my budding career as a chart reader I was taking classes at the Berkeley Psychic Institute. Twice a week I commuted to the Palo Alto branch, where my classmates seemed to be learning to be psychic quicker than I. Each week they reported seeing auras, chakras and past lives. As more and more of them opened their third eyes, I felt left in the dark.

Every time a student or teacher 'read' me, they gave the same report: My inner rose of clairvoyance had closed petals, the colors of my aura were dim, my higher consciousness was blocked.

As weeks turned to months I grew weary of hearing this, and felt as if everyone was advancing into some exotic country I couldn't enter. When I gazed at fellow students or teachers, instead of seeing auras I saw people gazing back at me.

I couldn't tell if my lack of progress was due to a flaw in my nature, a problem with the program, a failing in the faculty, or if the whole thing was full of shit to begin with. I knew it wasn't for lack of trying.

That morning, with the sliding glass door above the balcony open to the fresh California breeze, sitting on the bed, shirtless, meditating, with my back against the wall, I opened my eyes, looked down and saw colored spheres spinning.

In *me*.

Like a vertical column of suns, each a different multicolor, those radiant globes shimmered and spun and sparked plasma trails.

It took a long moment for me to realize I was seeing my chakras.

Until then I'd only seen chakras on posters and in books. But it was hard to relate two-dimensional images from old yoga books to these radiant globes. Those diagrams had made me think of chakras as disks; for some reason I'd never thought of them as spheres.

Later in my mystic apprenticeship I learned that one way to distinguish a clairvoyant vision from an imaginary experience is if the vision lies beyond the purview of anything you'd concoct. In other words, if you were writing a book, you'd never think to put that kind of scene in, because your imagination doesn't run that way.

Before you have an experience like this, it's hard for someone else to describe it in a way that does justice, because imagining you're seeing something is much different than seeing something. How I saw those spheres was how I see my computer screen now. There was nothing vague or blurry. I hadn't smoked ganja, drunk alcohol or taken drugs. I was stone-cold sober. The birds were chirping, the stream was gurgling, the day was fresh, sweet and California-clear—and there were these multi-colored suns, spinning and sparking.

Time stopped.

The air grew still.

Rather than concluding I'd gotten pranked by some wiseass at the institute who telepathically planted chakras in my head to keep my tuition money flowing, it seemed the opposite: I began to feel *undrugged,* as if the Thought Police failed to slip enough Ritalin into my food supply, and I was gazing through the thin surface of reality to what always lives below.

I leaned back into the wall, mouth agape, then began trembling.

It was one of those moments I'd seen in movies, where the wardrobe opens, the tornado drops, the universe pivots before settling into some new shape that suspiciously looks a lot like how it used to be, but is completely different.

Which made me wonder: How many ideas I've been relegating to fiction are fact?

How many worlds are hidden in plain sight?

What's the universe made of?

And—if I can see *this,* how many other things am I not yet seeing?

Staring at those multicolored suns, it dawned on me that most people don't see chakras not because chakras are imaginary, but because *most people don't see chakras.*

Inner vision isn't supported by society, isn't taught in grade school. Conversations with imaginary friends are frowned upon after age four.

When my third eye opened, it found me not in class but alone, and I'll be forever grateful it did, because to this day it remains one of the two most extraordinary experiences of my life, and there was no one else present to get between me and it.[19]

---

[19] The other was when my three-year-old son slammed head-first into the corner of a wooden deck that stopped his rocketing sled at the bottom of a steep, icy hill. The impact dug a two-inch crease an inch into his forehead that my wife Marcella was not going to

Eastern spiritualists would say my *kundalini* rose, to the extent that it took me the rest of that day and night and several more days and nights to slip far enough back into my customary self to barely begin fathoming what this meant, and how many other awakenings I'd have to go through before I awakened.

Sometime later—I don't know how long because it seemed both an eternity and much too brief—the sparking globes vanished and my torso reverted to skin. I was afraid to move in case they were going to come back.

They didn't but I know they're still there.

As I was to infer from subsequent visions, the powers that rule these things seem interested in peeling the curtains back for me one time only per extraordinary event. I think this is because it's up to me over time to figure out what to do with such gateways, how to mine their deeper layers and make the most of them, rather than craving for the curtains to keep peeling back again and again to assure me of extra dimensions or suit my spiritual ego. Little by little, over the years, I've had to allow my map of the Multiverse to fall into place with each new locale that gets shown to me, while leaning on mystery for all the rest.

If my vision had switched on at the institute, my name would've been added to the class list and I would've gotten patted on the back. But compared to those spinning globes, back pats seemed absurd. Like Dorothy Gale in Kansas, I'd been blown out of black-and-white into color, and knew I'd never go back.

After that morning I went through a 180-degree turn regarding metaphysics. Prior to then I'd regarded things like chakras, auras and past lives as wishful thinking, and things like consensus modern reality as rocksolid. Now I see it opposite: *Reality, as most people think of it, is the biggest hallucination of all.*

Like a papier-mâché construct, many layers thick, pasted around a magical planet that's a living being, we dwell in an existence several levels

---

allow to exist. It was the dead of winter, we were in a remote Airbnb far from the nearest hospital. Seconds after she picked him up and cradled him, his forehead popped out like a dent on a car. Afterward there was no blood, bump or bruise—as if it had never happened. Of my many mystical experiences, these two top the bill.

removed from the primal source of our thriving blue-green world, until a rupture in the construct opens a channel to all that's underneath.

It's not abnormal to see chakras. It's not abnormal to dream things before they happen. It's not abnormal to conduct telepathic conversations. It's not beyond belief to speak with the dead. What's beyond belief is how many people go about a blinkered version of reality and think they're seeing the whole thing.

To open a similar channel to the one that opened for me, if you find a willing partner you can try an exercise I call Eye-gazing:

Sit opposite your partner. Gaze into each other's left eye.

Let your breath relax and vision soften. Have no agenda but to see.

In my workshops, within minutes the face of the other person begins to soften and blur, flashing other features. In some of my private astrology readings, which is where I first witnessed this, faces I associate with the person's past lives dance across their current face. It's hard not to feel voyeuristic at these times, as if I'm spying on something far more personal than someone's naked body: their naked soul.

Sometimes another face takes over their current face so completely I have to shake my head and blink to remember what they looked like when they walked in the room. Sometimes the dancing faces only partly cover the current face, as if different time zones are being reshuffled in a kind of reincarnational musical chairs.

Often the gender of a dancing face is opposite that of my client. Sometimes it's a different ethnicity or age. Sometimes a face radiates an erotic charge that heats the air between us, giving me the sense I'm witnessing someone who never got sexual satisfaction in their past lives and wants it bad.

I believe the exercise works because two people linking with the simple intention to *see* thrust open curtains in the shared psychic space, which activates perceptual faculties that get lazy from lack of use.

If you try eye-gazing, don't give up if nothing seems to happen. One reason it works in my workshops is it's supported by group think. If nothing develops after five or ten minutes, try later.

After that morning I decided not to return to the Psychic Institute, because I'd gotten what I needed and wanted to continue exploring on my own.

Not long after, I stumbled upon Rudolf Steiner, one of the most advanced psychics of the last hundred years, who said, "For each step you wish to advance along the mystical path, you must take three steps to become a better human being."

This became the metric I still use. I've learned that mystic visions can be profound, and since that morning I've had several others (though in recent decades they've become more rare than they were during my apprenticeship). But visions, no matter how exalted, shouldn't exempt you from fully showing up for your life.

From Steiner I decided it could be an asset more than detriment to climb the mountain of psychic power slowly, while learning to be a better person, a better lover to the woman I knew I'd hook up with someday, by caring more about the world around me than the one beyond, and by striving to learn my personal lessons with a measure of humility more than dazzling others with my psychic prowess. When the etheric zones are used to support your daily existence rather than escape its rigors, you gain the best of both worlds.

A Capricorn whose time has come can be awesome to witness, because years of soul-wrestling yield a mastery that, like with champion athletes, can make the game of life look easy. Rather than getting buried under the avalanche of responsibilities that often suffocates the mischievous goat, decades of wrestling inner and outer forces yield the secret superpower of this sign: Earth Magic that blends human desire with cosmic frequencies to manifest what you focus on.

With the supreme distinction of opening the final third of the zodiac, passing tests of ego, sexual temptation and professional jealousy charges Capricorn's battery to peak manifesting power, so that a spark of effort sent in the right direction might fire up a whole new world.

Years of testing, coming near the tail end of the zodiac, where this sign inherits the legacy of nine earlier signs, set the stage for a command performance that Capricorn's audience sees only the neat results of rather than the messy rehearsals that went into it.

Capricorn, like fine wine, is intended to reach peak as it ages. If decades of trying to live up to its mountainous potential while inevitably falling short fail to quell and instead inaugurate the full force of indomitable Capricorn spirit, the happy, healthy, mischievous, gamboling, sidestepping, romping, stomping, playful side of the goat takes over. Life becomes something to butt up against and bound off of, rather get caged in by or run away from.

The Capricorn journey is the one zodiacal trek that can't be faked or finessed. It has to be earned every step of the way. This is the sign with no shortcuts and, ultimately, no wasted motion. Clumsy moves and wrong turns that may have seemed absurd or disastrous at the time plunge you through wormholes that deposit you where you were always trying to go, but couldn't land there till you went your own crazy way for a few years (or lifetimes) and then came out of it to find yourself precisely where you need to be, with the addition of having learned gritty and magical lessons on detours you'd never have taken if your ego had its way.

In the next and penultimate stage of the zodiac, the view from the mountaintop will rise even higher and expand through the universe, as the demands of advanced selfhood give way to the cosmic initiation of the final two signs.

But here, amidst the hardscrabble boulders, crumbling ledges and alpine inclines of the mountain goat's assiduous climb, and down among the submerged reefs of the seagoat's rigorous dives, the gods of internal awakening and quantum physics usher the goat into the mastery of using everything, wasting nothing and making all things count.

The endgame of Capricorn's soul-wrestling is to produce ultimate belief in yourself while recognizing the self doesn't even exist. When life becomes something you're totally invested in and completely free of, Capricorn fulfills its destiny, then passes the torch to the sign of our times, Aquarius.

CAPRICORN DRAGONHEAD/CANCER DRAGONTAIL

From interdependence to self-sufficiency

With Cancer behind you and Capricorn ahead, you're departing from interdependence and heading toward self-sufficiency. You're here to be a new kind of leader, who leads by authenticity instead of ego, and helps others find their own way. Wielding this kind of power is rare. Few role models exist because you're becoming your own. You can tell you're on track when your search for mastery raises everything in its way, which is why your journey is so prolonged and gritty. To climb that mountain you're grasping the reins in a chariot of paradox drawn by goats and dragons: The farther you climb, the more you realize how much farther there is to go. The more you awaken, the more you realize how unawake you are. Once you learn it's taking so long not because you're incapable or off-track, but because the route you chose has no shortcuts, the rest of the road opens. You know you're getting close when the world starts giving you what you want not because you're forcing it to but because you can't stop loving it.

From self-sufficiency to interdependence

With Capricorn behind you and Cancer ahead, you're departing from self-sufficiency and heading toward interdependence. The urge to do everything yourself may be noble, but you've come back to summon the circle—which means flipping your foibles into a communal way of operating rather than stuffing them under a crab shell. No shame in feeling overwhelmed, delegating power or asking for help. In past lives you were a dominant figure, set apart and above. You came back to get down into a life based on your kinship more than your glory. Vulnerability may be scary but beckons your dragon to find its place in the world, rather than only flying high above it. The problem with powerful people is they cast a lot of unconscious shadow. The belonging you crave won't arrive till you decide what not to belong to. You'll know you've come home to your tribe by the way it feels, and by how willing those around you are to meet your frailty as much as your strength.

CAPRICORN DRAGONTAIL/CANCER DRAGONHEAD

Underneath everything else each of us knows, we know one fundamental truth, no matter how hard it is to stick with: We all live in the same world and play for the same team. We're all parts of each other.

Why this should be hard for anyone to acknowledge is a riddle that water bearers never seem to get to the end of. How individuals and institutions can't get this through their heads is beyond the ken of even Aquarian thinking, which is saying a lot.

Water bearers are born knowing that each individual isn't an isolated entity, but part of a larger organization, which could be called the original worldwide web, or, more true-to-scale, the greater galactic web of integrated circuits and living tissue.

Although Mercury, Venus, Mars, Jupiter, Saturn and the rest of our planetary siblings have independent natures and separate locales, they orbit the same star we do, balancing each other's gravity with their own. Though separated by millions of miles, the movements of one affect the others, and the movements of all together create a solar symphony choreographed to the motion of nearby planets and distant stars.

Because animals, plants and planets fail to speak English doesn't mean they fail to speak. The intelligence of plants is different from that of humans, but no less extraordinary. Insects use communication networks far more elaborate than those of Silicon Valley. Earth too has consciousness, which makes it more of a sentient being than insensate hunk of rock.

The orbit of planets around stars replicates the orbit of electrons around the nucleus of an atom. Whether we look far away or deep within, we contact the same design of harmonic elegance beyond the wildest dreams of the most advanced supercomputer, in which every individual sends messages to the whole, and the whole sends messages back.

Like thousands of winged swallows simultaneously pivoting through the sky, harmony is achieved when the movements of individuals align with the grand design. If a single swallow departs from the flock, the whole flock notices. If a single species on a lonely planet sinks into discord, that section of the tapestry starts to unravel.

Long ago the Age of Aquarius was prophesied to herald the arrival of what Sufis call "A True Human Being," as if the version we've seen thus far is the prototype of a more advanced model. Through the ages, the advanced model emerged here and there in the form of individuals who saw beyond the limiting paradigms of their time, and held the curtains open for the rest of us.

History's sporadic emergences of the advanced model were predicted to build to a mass emergence around the 1960s, when an outbreak of heart consciousness was foretold.

Enter Aquarius, because, like a jug filled with holistic awareness, Aquarius holds the truth of our interconnectedness and carries that sloshing brew down many blind alleys and dead ends before figuring out what to do with it.

Bridge-Building Misfits & Holistic Fools: The Aquarian Art of Crossing the Gap

PROPHESIES AND PREDICTIONS ARE DUBIOUS AND UNCERTAIN things at best. Even when sensible, hopeful and more-or-less accurate they're subject to tremendous misinterpretation both unconscious and deliberate. But let's say for the sake of the human race that the best Aquarian Age predictions are true, and we really are in the initial stirrings of humanity's greatest transformation from the dark ages to something brighter.

Zodiacal ages are 2,173 years, which indicates that here at its outset, the Aquarian Age can't be expected to bridge the gap between ignorance and enlightenment all at once. In fact, the current period might be called *The Age of Everything* But *Aquarius,* because the only way we can outgrow the illusion of separation is if it's dramatized on the world screen for all to see.

Such dramas are taking stage more and more in the Karmic Theatre of our time, where the obsolete program of *this-against-that* and *that-against-this* is limned in stark detail against proliferating weapons and diminishing resources. Underneath the perpetual war machine that now runs the world economy, the Aquarian revolution that shook society in the Sixties can appear as outdated as go-go dancers and water beds.

When holistic awareness surged through the Sixties in waves it conjured the counterforce of a dark undertow that I don't believe we've gotten free of. The idea of love, peace and cosmic consciousness taking over society scared the shit out of repressive forces that are clamping down even harder these days to prevent a similar outbreak.

In my work raising consciousness with people around the world I often meet with others who want more than anything to believe in a bright future but can't shake the nagging feeling that it's an impossible dream. To lift their spirits I have to contend with parts of myself that similarly feel stymied by everything in the way of Aquarius.

If we're to believe the dominant paradigms presented by *The New York Times*, Fox News, NPR, MSNBC and other mass media, there's scant chance for international multitudes awakening to the idea that we're all parts of each other. Rather than a revival of peace and love there's far more evidence for collecting canned food and building fallout shelters.

But underneath those headlines I feel the soul of the species stirring to break out of the false security of an artificial existence that has clamped down more and more since the Sixties. Perhaps the banners of freedom we carried back then were naïve, perhaps we were arrogant in believing we could change the world, but the joy and hope we shared were real, and our bursts of creative vision were contagious. It felt so damn good to be so alive, and that is what I miss most.

While we don't need to bring back the immature excesses of that earlier movement, we dearly need to reconstitute its deep aliveness and radical joy. Believing in something sweeping and whole that regenerates the species may be the largest leap any of us can now make to bring on the Aquarian future we launched back then.

As the bright progressive side of the early Aquarian Age struggles to rise from obsolete and divisive consciousness, we have to contend with its dark side: the worst excesses of Hive Mind, which prevent individuals from thinking for themselves.

Hive-mind thinking has reached Orwellian proportions these days, where super-polarized ideologies run rampant and the idea of someone in the opposite camp having anything worthwhile to say is instantly stanched by thought police who monitor social media to quell outbreaks of original thought. University professors who dare say something that triggers the sensitive feelings of a single student get kicked out of school.

Public figures who mention an idea counter to their corporate sponsors are threatened with reputation smearing or jail time.

In the Sixties the arch-conservative William F. Buckley, Jr. ferociously debated liberal darling Norman Mailer in a series of public and televised debates where they went at each other's throats, but afterward would go on fishing trips with each other and their wives. Imagining that kind of cross-cultural camaraderie during today's political witch-hunts is nearly impossible.

A new puritanism has descended on collective thought, with people being afraid to say or think something different from their herd, in which social media popularity trumps independent thought. The same Aquarian holism that unifies individuals for evolutionary purposes has a dark side that entraps people in shallow polarized thinking while making them feel good about themselves because everyone around them thinks the same way.

So long as we cling to a herd identity that aggrandizes our side of the fence while demonizing the other, we're not going to reap the progressive interconnectedness of the Aquarian Age, because regardless of how pure and noble our affinity group may seem compared to the others, we're still stuck in the hyperpolarized consciousness threatening to break the world apart.

Somewhere between the obsolete paradigm of elite individuals ruling the rest of us, and the worst excesses of group mind dominating individual thought, the Water Bearer is calling us toward a new model that merges independent thought with collective consciousness for the good of the whole.

I confess that of all zodiac signs, this one is hardest for me personally to live up to. I have no planets in Aquarius, and so far as merging with the collective, my adolescent experiences in that direction left a lot to be desired.

After my early years in New York my family moved to Connecticut where I felt like a fish out of water. Though not religious, we were Jewish and most families around us were Catholic or Protestant. Even when I wasn't being called a Christ-killer I could always feel the difference.

I got turned on by poetry, mythology and writing; many of the boys around me were into sports and, as they got older, working on cars. I felt intimidated by sports and mechanics, as if the aptitude for them were a skill possessed by every other male but me. I was a little guy with a big mouth, which didn't endear me to tougher kids from Irish and Italian families whose parents were cops and mafia. I got ganged up on, jumped and beaten more than once before I began playing football and learned to fight back.

My way of coping with that ostracism and violence was to internalize the situation by telling myself, 'Everyone thinks there's something wrong with me—therefore there's something wrong with *them.*'

Since those years, if there's something that everyone else is doing I usually assume it's wrong. Despite all the work I've done on myself through astrology and psychedelics, and the growth I've achieved through love relationships, becoming a father late in life (I had my first child when I was almost fifty) and therapy, this is a hard habit to shake.

Though I feel a strong affinity with the part of Aquarius that has to do with overthrowing old models of separation, I find myself always reserving the right to think for myself and still harbor distrust of going along with the crowd. In this respect I may be more of a holdout from the previous Piscean Age than a full-fledged member of the new era.

During the Piscean Age religious salvation was in the hands of priests and kings, whereas in the Age of Aquarius we're due to claim full responsibility for our own enlightenment, which I do. The sleeping beast of collective consciousness is supposed to be awakening now, but I haven't found any social movement, political party or religious group that grabs me enough to give my love and loyalty to.

As a teenager I was a hippie, and proud of it. I sold hashish to work my way through high school, hitchhiked to California, dropped acid and followed the music. I scrutinized song lyrics and album covers while catching up on current events through long rap sessions in church coffee houses and street corners with other hippies I met while thumbing around the country. More than in school, I learned what life was like on the road.

In the South, as a long-haired young hippie, I got rides from truck drivers and state cops, tobacco-chewing good ol' boys, buttoned-down salesmen, schoolteachers, Marines and teenagers on their way to score pot. I learned that there's no one kind of person to trust and one not to, and that there's so much more good out there than bad.

Like most Sixties radicals I believed in Malcolm, Martin and Bobby while watching them get mowed down by the Machine, and for the sake of my children, recently mustered up a similar passion for Bernie Sanders until I watched him get dissed by his political bosses. I no longer believe any politicians are going to pry us out of the current dead end, or that any ism old or new (besides love-ism) is ever going to make a difference.

Even in my work as headmaster of The College of Visionaries & Wizards, which I run with my wife Marcella Eversole, where I conduct our three-year program that teaches people around the world how to read birth charts the soulful and magical way I do, I'm careful to warn my students not to look at astrology as the be-all and end-all of existence, but as a weaving of stories to help them develop their own stories. Rather than taking everything I say as gospel, my students are encouraged to test my ideas, challenge my assertions, try on for size the paradigms I offer and find their own truths.

A main reason I teach this way is because I'm aware of the tendency for any system, however high-minded or magical, to turn into a trap. Since my teens I've probably gained more consciousness from entheogens than anything else, but I'm aware of their dark side too. Drugs, religion, astrology, sex—even books—can open doors to higher consciousness or plunge you into paradigm prisons. My iconoclastic nature makes me an unusual astrologer: At the same time I sing the praises of starwork I warn my students not to get stuck there.

Many astrology-minded folks are shocked to learn that I haven't memorized the birth charts of my wife or children. I don't refer to astrology each day or consult the movements of the planets. I don't check the stars every time I schedule a podcast, the reason being that if astrology is real then it's already built into the fabric of everything.

If the stories I've been exploring in this book are actual forces at work in the cosmos, then since I'm part of the cosmos, those forces are already working in me. By digging down into the parts of me where those forces live, I ought to be able to arrive at the same place others get to without having to consult the stars. And if astrology is not already written into the fabric of the cosmos, if the ideas I've been playing with are entirely manmade, there's even less reason to memorize my kids' charts.

One of my favorite astrology anecdotes has to do with Rudolf Steiner, who most people don't think of as an astrologer because he's more well-known as the founder of Waldorf Education and the author of dozens of books that have nothing to do with astrology. Apparently a colleague approached Steiner and said, "I've noticed you scheduling your most sensitive and important talks on days of Mercury retrograde. Why would someone who knows as much of astrology as you know do something like that?"

Steiner reputedly smiled and said, "If I don't turn those energies around, who will?"

That's my kind of astrology.

Our uncanny blue-green garden planet is capable of generating life on a massive scale, clearing the decks, then starting over, as it has done a handful of times since the world began. But here's the catch: Every drop of water that existed in the beginning is still here. We breathe the same air the first protozoa breathed and drink the same water. There's no reserve tank. If we foul our nest beyond repair, there'll be nothing left to regenerate. But if recognition of our similarities trumps our fear of differences, we may avoid going the way of the tyrannosaur.

Growing up with a natural way of thinking that tends to be more unitive than the thinking of others around them, young Aquarians often get marginalized as the odd one out. Thus the Aquarian Paradox, in which the sign of interconnectedness can have the hardest time staying interconnected. Such ostracism may feel isolating in the short run but often plays better in the long run, as water bearers develop more of a universal citizenship than the neighborhood gang mentality in which our side is always homeboys and theirs is always scum.

By this advanced point in the zodiac its most complex forces seek expression. Along with next-door neighbor Capricorn, it takes Aquarians the longest time of any sign to come of age. Though they tend to see through limiting paradigms from adolescence on, water bearers need to undergo a lot of living to figure out what to replace them with. Only after trying many times to cram a multidimensional peg into a monodimensional hole are they likely to stumble upon a way of life that suits their rebel nature and inspires their holistic creativity.

Once found, they can tinker with that life vessel to their heart's content, and tinkering with paradigms delights this mad steampunk inventor of the zodiac as much as sex delights some other signs.

In the mystery school I stumbled into in 1990 in northern California, we were given a three-part blueprint of human consciousness, consisting of fate, karma and destiny:

Fate comprises the bulk of mass consciousness, which gets pushed around by external forces like a herd animal, barely waking up to your individual nature, tapping a fraction of your capacity.

Karma begins to awaken individuals out of the herd state, as you identify recurrent themes the universe sends you and learn to work with them, taking more personal responsibility and creative license for the way your life goes.

Destiny engages when your core ignites the dynamo of creative passion in you, springing your optimal future.

This paradigm is based on the idea of an organic living cosmos, in which several potential futures stream toward you any given moment, one being optimal, which may not manifest unless you latch onto it.

If you fail to latch on when destiny comes knocking, you may end up at a similar destination later. But then again, like a lover who wanted you long ago, before you could recognize the truth of what they were offering—that train may have left the station for good and your moment to combine with that particular future may have passed.

I've learned from decades of practicing astrology there are seasons of the soul, when a little bit of energy, applied in coordination with greater forces, goes a long way, yet that same energy exerted in some other time may fail to take you where you want to go.

Though the idea of destiny can have other meanings, in this paradigm destiny isn't passive but collaborative. Instead of referring to an irrevocable chain of events, it proposes a creative partnership: destiny as hunger to engage a stream of manifestation that the universe wants as much as you do.

I often contemplate the Aquarian-like consciousness that enables thousands of swallows or fish to pirouette, dip and rise as one, and wonder if there's a human equivalent.

Our mystery school breakdown of fate, karma and destiny offered us a map to steer by, and while it isn't the only possible map, the eleventh sign loves maps, schematics, blueprints and charts, which diagram the correspondence between micro and macro. I see Aquarians as the zodiac's cartographers, getting lost and found enough times to formulate their own eclectic subway maps of the universe.

Though they tend to pride themselves on analytical thinking, most Aquarians also have sharp intuition, which they may not recognize as intuition, because for them, like for Sherlock Holmes, it's simply elementary to see things that way. Like the famous Baker Street sleuth, many but not all people born in this sign worship logic and are skeptical of mysticism.

Whether they lean on logic or mysticism, I've been astonished by water bearers who instantly solve puzzles that confound me, as if privy to some mystic calculus they probably couldn't explain. They seem born to grasp the globularity of issues I get stuck in the clogged pipeworks of, which is why I call them cosmic plumbers.

Objectivity can be both boon and bane of this sign. Cold hard logic, when pushed to extreme (think of Mr. Spock in *Star Trek*) makes some Aquarians stiff, going through the motions rather than living from the heart. Their musculature tends to seize up around the neck, the part of the body that blocks the heart from the head. Since I heard Alan Watts satirize a businessman's tie as a symbol of Western-Civilization cutoff between thinking and feeling, when I walk down city streets at rush hour I can't help seeing ties as ugly blotches, like the kind they superimpose over handcuffed criminals' faces on newscasts.

Besides that neck block there's a freer version of Aquarian objectivity, not disconnected so much as non-attached, somewhat Buddhist, more relaxed. I believe the difference depends on the ratio of the warmth of their presence to the rigidity of their ideas.

Even when they warm up, though, inside every Aquarius lurks a scientist, and according to the traditional scientific method of thesis, antithesis and synthesis, ideas must be proposed in neutrality. The more unbiased the inquiry, the more it may produce the lovely and elegant syntheses Aquarians delight in, since probably even more than Scorpio they're the synthesis fiends of the zodiac.

Though he wasn't Aquarius but the subsequent sign, Pisces, the 19th-century astrologer-scientist-educator Rudolph Steiner gave us what may be the world's ultimate synthesis:

> When tempted to find an imperfection in the universe, you'll make progress if you assume the flaw is more due to your temporary failure to grasp the underlying web of unity that connects all things, rather than an actual imperfection.

Having worked with this idea for thirty years I've come to believe it takes the courage of the Fool in the tarot deck, about to blithely step off a cliff, to believe in a unifying principle so omnipresent it might be called love.

The beauty of Steiner's Web is it doesn't remove the onus for awakening from you and me. It doesn't advocate limp passivity or blind faith. It implores you to approach dysfunction and travesty as gaps in a greater unity you may be able to bridge by stretching your heart and mind.

Steiner's Web becomes practicable if we view the universe as a *being* more than a thing. As a thing, the universe is easy to typecast as having no particular reason to care about you or me or anything. As a being, it stands to reason that, like in a single human body, each part contributes something vital to the whole, and the strength of the whole depends on the efficacy of its parts.

There's support throughout your physiology for your kidneys to operate with maximum efficiency and minimum resistance, because then they drain less energy and produce more vital force to the whole system. It stands to reason kidneys work best when gallbladders, feet and hands do, and your gallbladder works best when your ankle does, and so forth throughout the integrated system. Each part has an independent function that contributes to the health of the whole, and the health of the whole strengthens the functionality of each of its parts. If one component goes out of whack, the others have to compensate.

If the body of the cosmos operates like human bodies, not so different in design, mostly different in scale, then when anything in the universe aligns with its optimal flow, the less drag it's going to cause on the rest of the system.

Perhaps every time any part of the universe fulfills its function with the least fuss and bother, the whole shebang runs more smoothly. And, like celestial acupuncture, if a planet somewhere on a meridian gets blocked, the stimulation of another point on that same meridian might clear the blockage.

Due to their natural inclination toward integrated systems, for some Aquarians the self, as most of us know it, barely exists. This sign is located as far as the zodiac gets from selfhood and ego, which is the dominion of Leo, on the opposite side of the wheel.

Water bearers are born knowing they themselves are not the issue. The issue is how they plug into a greater system. Sure, it's crucial to take care of yourself, stay healthy and thrive, but when you perform those functions inside a thriving ecosystem, you contribute to the health of the whole and draw sustenance from it.

In the prior stage it was Capricorn's job to wrestle the gnarly human ego into shape. When Aquarius grabs the torch it's poised to take the zodiac in a whole new direction. It's not up to the penultimate sign to somehow build up human selfhood even more but to transform it to a fluid vessel.

The eleventh sign is the zodiac's melting-pot, whose universal awareness enables it to understand many things without needing to think about them. Aquarians see across gaps others get lost in and pop out syntheses without working up a sweat. If and when anyone else will cross those gaps is another issue, which is why it can get kind of lonely out there on the Aquarian bridge-building crew. Like a mutational cell going off in a progressive direction it's no sure bet if and when the rest of the cells will follow.

It's unusual to find Aquarians settling down much before their fifties, because till then they tend to spend as much time trying on lifestyles as some folks spend trying on shoes. What to do, how to think, who to be with and how to make money are questions others tend to resolve earlier in the game.

A great turning point occurs in the Aquarian journey when they define themselves more by what they fit *into* than what they're breaking out of. Instead of forever playing rebel without a cause like Aquarian James Dean (though in the movie he actually had a very good cause), they find or create a vessel to channel their rampant energies, which can make all the difference.

The evolution of an Aquarian is like the slow gestation of a collage out of ragtag pieces of experience. Only when enough pieces have been spread on the table can the composite emerge. Until then this sign often collects experiences that are awesome but keep shuffling and unshuffling before they add up.

People born in this sign often report dreams of being chased, which makes me wonder what's pursuing them: The Monster of Reality? The Fearsome Specter of a world without unity? The creeping feeling they're not as free as they should be? Perhaps the chase stimulates the part of them that longs to get seduced but hasn't yet found a sufficiently enticing seduction.

Aquarians seem to have the most unusual relationship to electricity. With nothing in their pockets they set off body scanners and bookstore alarms. I think this is because like a human satellite dish they relay so many energies that some are bound to short-circuit, which places a premium on vigorous physical activity to ground their operations.

When stressed, water bearers are more likely to blow a mental fuse than have emotional breakdowns. Rather than screaming, they tend to skew their perspective, staring into something wrong and insisting it's right, or the other way around.

This sign also seems unusually wired to its dreams, handling the vast bulk of its tasks while asleep. I imagine Aquarians clocking in their main occupation when their heads hit the pillow, and punching the clock for quitting time when they wake.

My Aquarian lovers took long to emerge from sleep. Like an interrupted hibernating bear, they seemed to come back begrudgingly, as if compared to their nocturnal sojourns, life in the physical plane is just too clunky to bother with. Some seem to resent their humanness as if it's the booby-prize for failing to reach Nirvana when they reincarnated from spirit and landed in the material plane by accident.

Which brings us to the Aquarian body. My main intimacy with Aquarian bodies is the female variety because I've had more Aquarian lovers than any other kind, who seemed unusually susceptible to pleasure, as if it takes over not just their body but their whole being. Like the vessel of its water-bearing namesake, the Aquarian body seems to be particularly receptive to being filled by something pouring into it.

I saw similar events in movie theaters, where my lovers' gasps and grimaces indicated they lacked the ability to separate themselves from the film pouring into them. I envy but also fear that empathic receptivity, because no matter how much I adore a movie, I never forget I'm in the theater watching it. My New-York-born, Scorpio-fueled, Capricorn-based survival instincts are not likely to merge with characters on the screen to the extent that I completely forget myself.

The poet Ezra Pound said artists are the antennae of the race. I think he meant if humanity were an insect, artists would get wherever we're going first, and relay messages of what they find back to the main body. He might've been talking about Aquarians like Galileo, Darwin,

Lincoln, Susan B. Anthony, FDR, Rosa Parks, Hank Aaron, Bob Marley and Thomas Edison.

Aquarius rules acupuncture and acupressure, eye iridology and foot reflexology, bio-kinesthetic maps that demonstrate how separate parts are connected in a living system. If you have a problem with your liver, a needle in your leg might clear the same circuit. Wouldn't it be fantastic if, instead of global competition, Russia was seriously stuck and we needled Washington, DC, to clear the channel?

Just as the lion on the opposite side of the zodiac is stalking self-actualization, Aquarius is stalking the greater awareness sleeping in our species.

If the idea of collective awakening seems like a leftover hippie dream, remember that quantum physicists tell us the way we look at something may change it. That means your and my thoughts, which are probably alchemically blending now that you've made it this far into the book, might redirect the universe.

As an isolated entity you may not have much say. As a living cell in the greater galactic web, the whole universe might have a hell of a lot to say through you.

After humanity vanishes, life will go on.

The day our sun dies, new stars will be born.

Galactic watchers might one day say: "Humanity rose from its delusions of separation to claim its true nature in the nick of time. Gaia had been a blocked acupuncture point on the galactic meridian for far too long. That corner of the cosmos had grown toxic. Human awakening cleared the channel and released trapped energies. As their planet swept back into orbit the entire system began to work better."

AQUARIUS DRAGONHEAD/LEO DRAGONTAIL

From individuality to collectivity

With Leo behind you and Aquarius ahead, you're departing from individuality and heading toward collectivity. Your past lives featured the blessing and curse of big selfhood, which granted you strength of character but resistance to merging. That strength can thicken to a skin of ego that prevents love from getting in and soul from getting out. You got fed up with counting on anyone who wasn't you, and that's a tough habit to break. The good news is allies are everywhere because even if you feel squashed down on the planet, your Aquarian Dragonhead grazes the ceiling of the universe. Most people speak Earth talk; you've come to decode the cosmos. The awakening of our time needs spiritual outlaws to subvert the dominant paradigm, overthrow the Rule of Ego and bring on the Rule of Love. The more you refuse to get drafted into the Polarity Wars, the more you help bring about *The End of Everything That Never Worked Right in the First Place,* by building a bridge from this strange modern disconnect to the unified field beyond, where dragons romp.

From collectivity to individuality

AQUARIUS DRAGONTAIL/LEO DRAGONHEAD

With Aquarius behind you and Leo ahead, you're departing from collectivity and heading toward individuality. You gained past-life experience learning to think the way others thought, which postponed the full release of creative forces packed in you. Having been insufficiently tapped through the ages, that spiritual bank account accrued interest. As soon as you're ready, you can draw from vast funds, but the kicker is you have to know you're ready rather than just be kind of ready. You've got to get out of your own way. Your dragon is sitting on heaping mounds of creativity that await your willingness to be the absurdly flawed individual you are. Trust what you love and can't live without and let the rest go. Some throwaway ideas you let slip by might yield a whole life. The lion of your soul knows what it's after, but it's taking a while for the rest of you to catch on.

CHAPTER TWELVE

More than anything, Pisces wants to play. Pisces wants to usher you into the festival that life becomes when you enter it that way. But each time it swims that direction it rarely gets far before crashing into the great barrier reef of conscience.

So much needs to be done, so many things are in disarray, that Pisces knows each time it goes off to play it could instead be cleaning the mess. Lord knows no one else is. Or if they are, they're cleaning the surface of the mess while ignoring the deeper mess down below that Pisces would love to ignore but just isn't built that way.

To sail around the reef and keep swimming is what Pisces longs to do, for who wouldn't choose leaping through frothy waves over cleaning sticky messes?

But to go that way means abandoning the mess to the uncertain custodianship of others, where it's bound to defy incomplete cleaning and, soon as Pisces's back is turned, could mutate into something messier.

Pisces wants to swim on but knows that few others are as adept at cleaning messes. So there, in the lee of the barrier reef, Pisces sighs a deep sigh, as if it's been getting caught in messes far too long to find any easy way out but can at least do what Pisces does best—hope.

There's no sigh quite like a Piscean sigh, no eyes so moist and eloquent, no sign that eclipses this one when it comes to hope. But it's the kind of hope that can only arise at the end of the zodiac, the hope of a seafarer long adrift to return to the long-lost comfort of home.

Islands in the Storm: The Long-Heralded, Much-Delayed, Piscean Art of Arrival

AND SO WE ARRIVE AT THE END OF OUR JOURNEY. AFTER ALL other signs have fallen like rain upon the earth, we come to the sea. After each art has had its say but one, we launch the ultimate art: holding true to yourself in the oceanic intensity of everything life throws at you.

If you stand fast in that storm, you'll arrive in the Mississippi delta of the zodiac, where eleven rivers pour into the sea, and instead of being swept away by the Incarnation Blues, you'll gain the soulful presence the whole progression has been leading to.

Until now the only sign that's gone this deep is Scorpio, but Scorpio's depth is that of an underground river while the depth of Pisces is that of the sea.

Till gaining that ultimate soulful presence, you'll flicker through the world in stolen moments like a shadow puppet, while your real life moves some other way down below.

How did we get so split?

In childhood we start out living the life of the soul because we don't know anything different but then get shanghaied by social forces pressing us into service, and we begin to diverge from our inner compass, often ending up in lives far from the one our ruby heart and dragon's head are aiming for.

Since Pisces is the zodiac's oceanic metamorph, when coercive forces come knocking, it sends a very capable part of itself out to adapt to the ways of the world but holds back a deeper part, which gets buried like pirate gold.

The return of that buried treasure is the final quest of the zodiac.

Underneath its emotional waves, transitory needs and passing fancies, Pisces is searching for its missing piece.

During the search, Pisces is weaving a warp of desire through a weft of compassion, creating the basket of hope it uses to petition higher powers to grant humanity a chance to outgrow its delusion that anything is more important than love.

Pisces is the zodiac's *ancient child,* striving, despite everything it has witnessed, to give its all to existence.

The Piscean part of you is out to learn how with everything you know about our miraculous planet and mixed-up species, you can still put it all on the line and give it your best shot; how in a world of departures you can somehow arrive.

If you find the *cojones* (or your gender equivalent) to be badass enough to fall in love with life like you did as a child—taking it all in, giving it all out, holding back nothing—the ancient part of you goes on a walkabout with the child part, to learn how innocence can be reborn in a lost world.

In its interlude by the reef, Pisces extends its electroreceptors— the highly developed sensors of a manta ray or a shark's Ampullae of Lorenzini, which enable them to precision-navigate Earth's magnetic field—to find if the way lies ahead or behind: Does the urge to go back and deal with the mess stem from higher wisdom or self-denial?

After Capricorn and Aquarius, this sign has a tough act to follow. These three, who inherit the evolutionary arc of the first nine, are where the fullest expression of the zodiac is intended to bloom.

Capricorn is the apex sign striving to enact its highest knowing, so Aquarius can expand human consciousness to the stars.

Pisces's task is to plunge the stellar waters of Aquarius down to the water of life itself. The eleventh sign, like a satellite dish, launches us up and out, while the twelfth, like a massive sea creature, dives us down and in to marry the truth of our intentions to the integrity of our actions.

Such a tremendous wedding ushers this sign through many changes, both its own and that of others, for Pisces has about as much chance of remaining separate as a raindrop does of staying separate from the sea.

At this point everything the zodiac had to teach about separation has come and gone, because after Pisces, Aries is coming, and for individuation to start all over again, as when sperm meets egg, it has to be born from a merged state, which is one of many reasons Pisces is so merge-y.

Pisces is the electromagnetic sea of impressions we dive into when we come back from spirit for another go at life. It's the world ocean, the swirling karmas, the pressures of the deep, which after the freedom of the disembodied state, submerge the soul in the rigors of reincarnation.

Until the final sign dissolves every barrier between it and existence, it's clinging to driftwood, seizing fragments rather than doing what it was born to do—plunge into the bottomless embrace the sea of life holds for humanity.

To pull off the zodiac's ultimate quest demands dogged perseverance and a huge heart, which is why this old sea dog tends to be as wry and salty as it is gullible and sincere.

Although the zodiac's maximum expansion occurs in the last two signs, they have very different ways of going about it. Aquarius tends to be airy and detached, expanding the networks of consciousness more than the visceral realms of feeling. Pisces tends to be more primal, and so *non*-detached, that as its feelings expand it often feels responsible for things no other sign would, as if the folly of the species is something it must personally account for.

The tension between Pisces's urge to serve and its yearning to be free is symbolized by its glyph, which depicts two stylized fish swimming opposite directions, bound by a thin silver chain:

In its moment by the reef, if Pisces chooses to go back and deal with the mess, one fish will swim free while the other stays chained.

But if Pisces refuses to deal with the mess for reasons of self-comfort and emotional denial, the opposite fish will swim free while the *other* remains chained.

Opposing Pisces's urge to swim free is a fierce undertow of conscience that tells it to be reasonable, think about others, turn around, go back and deal with the mess.

To counter that undertow Pisces yanks hard in the opposite direction, which breaks the silver chain and releases the two fish. As the chain wafts toward the sea floor, let's see where they go.

Despite pinpricks by spiny urchins of conscience, when the chain breaks, the first fish resumes its journey, hell-bent (or heaven-bound) for the glorious festival. The urge to revel in existence, raw and dripping, and drink life to the dregs propels Pisces up from the depths to the surface like an onrushing whale, where it breaches, blowing off the steam of the unlived life.

Flapping its flukes away from altruistic self-sacrifice thrusts Pisces into a life that's like a prayer in motion. Like a force of nature, it plows ahead with the surge of a leviathan who draws everything in its wake.

Some of my most vivid and unforgettable moments have come from being drawn into the wake of intimate Piscean friends I swam the world with. Though their elemental wildness and sudden changes upended my life and flung me into roiling seas, they showed me what it means to be alive. It was a Pisces stoner friend who talked me into leaving my family in Connecticut and hitchhiking to San Francisco with him when I was sixteen, plunging us into the tidal aftermath of the Sixties, and though I returned back east at the end of that summer, I was never the same.

Coming at the end of the zodiac lends Pisceans the air of old souls, who've seen so much in one life or other that little in this life could shock them. Them getting shocked is probably the only thing that could shock them.

When you're an ancient child you've seen what human beings do to each other, but even so, the innocent part of you learns to keep arriving fresh all over again, as if you can't stop believing something wonderful is about to happen.

One of the best-kept secrets of our species—though it's not so secret from Pisces—is we can't stop believing something wonderful is about to happen.

As tough and gritty as this sign can be, it knows the best response to confounding dilemmas is to dive in, follow its heart and let its body take the blows, rather than treading water in a world without love.

Love is taking so long to happen in this world, a soul, in fact, might be let off the hook for thinking it never will. But that's a luxury Pisces can't afford, because if the most hopeful sign throws in the towel, we're all up shit creek without a paddle.

The surge of the breaching whale floods back to the reef, where the second fish is still trying to make up its mind. In the midst of the backwash this one turns around and faces the way it came.

Although its heart leaps at the idea of partying at the festival, the second fish senses its path lies elsewhere, toward the plausibility of a conscience well-appeased and a job well-done, which requires getting tangled in some net it can't untangle without first getting caught in.

So, after that eloquent sigh, instead of primal release the second fish swims into the net.

Pisces is the sign for which every pull has a counter pull, every spring tide has a neap tide, and each gain comes at a cost. The cost for choosing to deal with the mess is the postponement of freedom. The party's over, or will be by the time Pisces gets there, but as much as this sign yearns to play, it hungers for something beyond cheap thrills.

The rightfulness of this choice hinges on whether it's driven more by love or martyrdom. When Pisces takes a job it'll scour the seven seas to get it done, but if self-flagellation rather than self-truth drives its fury to clean, it'll generate internal messes while mopping up external ones.

No other sign has such easily accessible surfaces and unapproachable depths. None is so immensely powerful and so frequently lost at sea.

The other eleven are rivers pouring into the twelfth's marine basin, filling it with myriad ways to be, because Pisces, possibly even more than Gemini, is the zodiac's champion shapeshifter.

When you're that metamorphic, what to do with freedom is an ongoing concern. And what to do with freedom when few others are free is an even bigger one.

Often, what Pisces does is find some new net to get tangled in, so it can focus its often-scattered energies on untangling, and so it can avoid parading its freedom in front of those less fortunate.

Choosing which way to go is an ongoing initiation for this sign, who's packed with so many forces craving expression that it's often afraid of blowing people away. That's not usually a conscious fear, though, because few Pisceans realize the extent of what they're carrying. But even the strongest sign can't hold back the tide.

When you can be anything, you spend a lot of time being nothing. This is a downstream kayak glide if you're ready to handle it, but an upstream salmon fight if you're not.

Like a tsunami, Pisces is the one sign that can't be stopped once it's fully mobilized and on track. But it takes so much to get Pisces fully mobilized and on track that most never do. Until then it lacks a rudder, and the most powerful sign is everywhere and nowhere, hurtling past island after island without making landfall.

I believe Pisces is the most cinematic sign, whose life unfolds in a series of comic and dramatic images more than via sequential logic. Filmmakers, graphic artists, comic book writers and artists, actresses, directors and dancers operate along these lines.

I see Pisces akin to poetry more than prose, because unlike articles or essays, the piscine journey seems to proceed less by analytic rationale than by poetic leaps that may not make sense at the time, but carry some deeper truth that may become evident later. Or not.

One of the greatest zodiacal ironies is the ultra-fluent member of the zodiac can't be budged once it gloms onto purpose. Until then it bobs around like a jellyfish in a typhoon, but heaven and earth would be easier to dislodge than a Pisces whose mission has arrived.

Because eleven rivers pour into the Pisces sea, this sign is teeming with vast superworlds waiting to burst into life. Not because they're empty do Pisceans suffer, but because of the fullness they carry without knowing where to put it.

Lacking adequate outlets, Pisces can grow bloated as a blowfish with corked passion, and sink into emotional funks, where they often pine for someone to come to their rescue, until realizing they need someone to *give to* more than take from. They need a pure form of giving, though, that exceeds neediness and guilt.

Regarding the two fish swimming opposite directions, this sign paradoxically has the least and most self-confidence in the zodiac. Because Pisces rarely trusts others to handle things as thoroughly as it can, it has massive conviction, but flimsy ego and little sense of its own capacity, because how do you measure the sea?

It's an astrological cliché to say Pisces is susceptible to drugs and drinking, but there's truth there, because a sign this vulnerable often wears its heart on its sleeve, feeling things so nakedly it has extra temptation to go comfortably numb.

The weight of the world, like the phenomenal pressure at the bottom of the ocean, lies heavy on the last sign, whom even in its relaxed moments seems to be wrestling some existential dilemma—or maybe not. Maybe that melancholy isn't circumstantial but the natural feeling tone of an old soul.

I envision the archetypal Pisces as having liquid, knowing eyes, and hands palm-out as if to say, 'Yeah, I know—life sucks. This world is a fucking madhouse with a rare flower inside. We all suffer from trapped love, but can we get it together one more time to pluck the flower?'

Because it's not easy for an oceanic shapeshifter to know whether to cling like a barnacle or leap like a dolphin, Pisceans tend to vacillate between being gloriously easygoing and stubbornly controlling.

Pisceans almost always have an abundance of friends, but sometimes feel isolated, because few meet them in the place they crave to be met. Rarely is it a challenge for Pisces to make social connections. Almost always it's a challenge to reduce the amount of people who want to connect with them to the ones they want to connect with. Until then, fishes often swim through the unenviable condition of being over-accompanied and under-met.

Though they can suffer a lack of intimacy, it's not always sex they need but authentic camaraderie.

To constantly change is like never changing because it's constant, so to swim with companions of the soul can provide continuity for this chameleonic octopian, and may catapult the often-shy and unassuming final member of the zodiac to the life of the party.

Though they can have the hardest time fathoming their own natures, most Pisceans have canny instincts regarding the natures of others. If you can get a fish past politeness into candor, you may be blown away by how well they read people.

But those sharp perceptions may get muddied in the rigid assumptions they're often hooked by. Fish tend to jump to so many conclusions and make so many snap judgments it's not a bad idea to pick up a Pisces every so often and throw it in a lake. After all that saltwater, some fresh currents might do them good.

Like the ocean, Piscean consciousness waxes and wanes more than staying the same. The likelihood of life going one way for long for a Pisces is about the same as it is for the tide to only come in. Love, health, flow of feelings, work, play, mental clarity and sex, like all things Piscean, ebb and flow through drastic extremes.

When they're clear and on track Pisceans tend to be pristinely clear and gloriously on track. And when they're off track they tend to be gloriously off, requiring someone obstinate as they are to get through to them (which may be hard to find).

Amid its currents and counter-currents, the twelfth sign possesses a little-known power: a magnetism that draws out the true nature of others the way rivers are drawn to the sea. Few Pisceans are aware of this quality, which differs from most personal magnetism, where one person is captivated by another's magnetic pull. In this version, Pisces, without necessarily doing something specific, conjures a fuller experience out of others.

For a sign that gets swept through so many changing tides, sometimes art is the only thing that keeps them sane, like Pisces George Harrison crying:

> Give me love
> Give me love
> Give me peace on earth
> Give me light
> Give me life
> Keep me free from birth
> Give me hope
> Help me cope, with this heavy load
> Trying to touch and reach you with
> Heart and soul

Through such artistic outpouring, the saltwater of Piscean tears can get transmuted to a wine of ecstasy. The difference between an ecstatic fish and a moping one can be breathtaking. So much is always pouring *into* Pisces that when its inner richness starts pouring out, everyone in the vicinity is likely to get drenched.

The surface of this sign can be the blandest in the world, and least indicative of what's going on below. And what's going on below depends on which layer you look at. How many micro-climates exist between the top and bottom of the sea?

The deepest region is populated by the strangest creatures on Earth, who glide through the blackness like prowling aliens. It can be difficult for Pisces to keep track of what's going on down there till someone switches on a floodlight, which can be risky. As my friend Dawn, who sailed across the Atlantic in a small boat, likes to say, the ocean has a million ways to kill you.

Even if you can't see what's going on in Piscean depths, you can infer it from their eyes, which gaze into the world as if from deep-water caves. Often hooded, they seem to squint and cogitate like old fishermen. Few signs can look so placid and feel so volatile.

Due to its position of honor at the end of the zodiac, this sign contains a little bit of each of the others, which can make it easier for Pisces to understand them than for them to understand it. The fish is the one who sees but is seldom seen, and hears but is less often heard, which might make it lonely but can inspire it to find a depth of self that is commensurate with its deep feeling for others.

If you get intimate with a Pisces, you might hear them release a sigh, as if to say, 'So, you're crazy enough to come into my craziness? Uh, okay then, come in. I can't guarantee your safety, but if you ever make it back out, please fill me in on what's going on down there....'

When someone meets the parts of Pisces that hadn't been met, one of its greatest shapeshifts occurs. Like rubbing a magic lamp, when you make love to a Pisces, or make friendship, there's no telling what might come out. But whatever does, once it starts, it's not likely to stop soon because how do you stop the sea? Lovers seeking something safe and manageable should look elsewhere.

Unlike some lovers, Pisces doesn't want love's perks so much as love's realness, and needs less sugar-coated reassurances than honest companionship and good hard loving. Though they often change direction and shift attitude, when that huge heart opens this sign can become dauntlessly steadfast.

If relationship dives deep enough, interior contents that Pisces was carrying but may not have been aware of start releasing from the depths, which can dump flotsam into choppy seas. Sometimes secrets Pisces carried alone in the dark reveal themselves for the first time in the act of giving them away. When you grasp something for the first time while giving it away, you're practicing death, a timely skill at the zodiac's last stop.

In the divine comedy of life, there's only one bedrock certainty: Sooner or later you're going to die. Everyone you know is going to die. Astronomers tell us one day the Sun will grow so big it'll swallow the Earth, and Earth will die. Or maybe we'll get hit by an asteroid before then.

Western civilization has never been good at death and dying because in a pharmacy-driven, youth-fixated culture, it tends to marginalize the event as if it only happens to losers.

Many people go through life pretending old age can be driven off by Viagra, hair plants and tummy tucks. When someone begins dying many people avoid them and pity them and their loved ones, as if death is shameful and contagious, and must be kept away from the living.

What's shameful isn't death but what we've done with it, turning life's most inevitable passage into something ghastly. While it's true some deaths are particularly grievous, especially death of the young, even those are best handled by confrontation rather than denial. In this way death is like a big cat—it loosens its grip on you once you stop running from it.

I found this out twenty years ago in San Diego, when my mother lay dying of lung cancer in the hospital where I sat with her day and night. As I held her hand for the first time in forty years, I was shocked by how soft it was, like a baby's bottom, rather than dry or wrinkled like an old person's, as I'd imagined it to be. I couldn't get over that silkiness.

At one point her skin turned translucent, releasing a rose-golden radiance that filled the room. The nurses saw it too. That glow melted walls that had kept us apart, which I hadn't known were there till they started melting.

I sat beaming unconditional love into her, which brought tears to my eyes as I realized this was the same love she must've beamed into me when I was newborn to the world she was now leaving.

talking in tongues

when i open my mouth   the words & feelings rush out so fast
                                i don't know what or when to do
                                with them & the blood pulses so fast
                                you're lying on the hospital bed
                                you're my mother & you're dying
                                you're my mother & you're dying
                                you're my mother & you're dying

when i open my mouth   cold fingers seize my organs making
                                me realize making me know making
                                me realize making me know how
                                much of my life i clench spent
                                clenching how much my life is
                                just clenched up
                                i hold back we
                                hold back i hold back my love

when i open my mouth   & see the nurse come shoot you
                                with 40 mg. of morphine stick you
                                pierce you prick you shoot you with
                                20 mg. shoot you with 40 mg. shoot
                                morphine into your delicate
                                hard-to-find veins that
                                dart & twist away from the needle

                                nobody can find you ma they bring
                                in needle experts they can't find
                                you either
                                your eyelids flutter
                                your veins retreat
                                your hands whisper above the bed
                                like a bird like an angel like a bird
                                like an angel like an angel of pain

when i open my mouth   everything i never said couldn't say
                                needing to say never known never
                                owned never known till now how
                                beautiful you are mom

why—why
does it take this
why couldn't i know
why couldn't i speak
why couldn't i know why couldn't i
see the flame that burns inside
me is your flame?

when i open my mouth   all i can say
is i love you.

i love you and i'm here.

i'm here.
& i love you.

i'm here.

& after a day & a night & a night & a day of you sinking
into coma not talking not speaking knowing what how
many things you know i never could tell
not speaking barely
breathing breath gasping clutching stopping——

& then starting.

and after every stop my heart stopping
exhale inhale *now*? not
now *now*? not now

after two silent days & nights the new night nurse comes in & stupidly
says how are you mrs. borax & & &
your eyes open & you
say "okay" as if you were crossing a street
so casually my jaw drops and i don't know how
to anything when you're my mother & i see!
i see you smile & i smile back & say
"hi, mom" & you say "hi, mark" & i now
know that for the rest of my life i can finally breathe.

Because in this mixed-up world death is the only certainty, it should be the least weird thing of all. Midwifing my mother's passage taught me that the dying need from us the same thing the living do, but even more, which is what Pisces has been swimming toward all along: the blazing realness of open-hearted presence.

Such arrival gives the departing one something solid to push off of, and heads off remorse that might overwhelm you later if you look back and realize you failed to show up for their departure.

Heraclitus said you can't step in the same river twice. Zen Buddhists say you can't catch running water in a bucket. Both could be talking about Pisces, whose cinematic flourishes and poetic leaps may come closest to capturing the dream of life our souls began dreaming when Earth summoned our bodies from the sea of incarnation.

Woven through its highly changeable, often grueling, sometimes ecstatic, mixed-up, muddled-up journey, Pisces knows the great secret that beneath everything else we came for, we came for love. And the only way to land there is to become present to the great love that already is, not just the one we keep looking for.

When Pisces no longer runs away from any of it, but stays strong and firm and lets the gales of incarnation wash over, the staunch, constant, fully-present-and-accounted-for, hard-loving, easily-swooning, true-blue, ocean-hearted, indefatigable arrival of this sign is the next shape it shifts into, and maybe the last.

After each stormy island has been left behind, and the shadow puppets dissolve into liquid moonlight, the sigh Pisces sighs has a much different tenor than the one it sighed when trying to make up its mind at the coral reef, because every direction now leads home.

248

PISCES DRAGONHEAD/VIRGO DRAGONTAIL

From the conditional to the unconditional

With Virgo behind you and Pisces ahead, you're departing from the conditional and heading toward the unconditional. This is an orgy of surrender, sure to raise everything impossible to surrender to until you make love with it. So many thought forms block us from merging with the love we're made of, but are those shadow puppets real? Love and hate...Me and you...Reality and magic...These are thick coral reefs you crash into until their boundaries blur and colonies merge and you find yourself back where you started from. Incarnation is teaching you how to get out of your way by first seducing you through every possible variation of getting *in* your way. No matter how fervently you chase perfection you'll never get there, not because there's something wrong with you, but because the human part of you will always be human, even as the dragon in you soars like a dolphin leaping toward the sun, before it jackknifes, surrendering to gravity, and plunges back into the world ocean.

From the unconditional to the conditional

PISCES DRAGONTAIL/VIRGO DRAGONHEAD

With Pisces behind you and Virgo ahead, you're departing from the unconditional and heading toward the conditional. This is the most exacting journey in the zodiac, with the most stringent demands, like passing a dragon through the eye of a needle. There's a way to live, a code to follow, a *feng shui* to practice, which can be found by becoming so true to your nature that you attune to the nature of all things. There's a purity in you dying to come out. If you push that with rigid dogma, it'll trap you, because you came to gain acute devotion more than anybody's ism. Like harnessing an ocean, this task is so monumental that sometimes all you can do is howl at the cosmic jest of having chosen to be human during a time of great chaos and confusion. Everything comes back to your body. Once your body leads you to the dance you were born to dance many things you thought were impossible fall into place, and, minus a few claw tips and shredded scales, your dragon emerges on the other side of the needle.

Afterword:
The Flight of
the Dragon

MANY PEOPLE ASSOCIATE ASTROLOGY WITH PREDICtion, but the soul-level version of the art that I created in 1987, which I practice in private sessions and teach in The College of Visionaries & Wizards, is more about identifying your authentic nature than telling you what's going to happen. It's about peeling off layers of conditioning, prying away false stories and freeing your destiny.

I believe your soul took a body to express the enormous love packed into it. That love is the hope of humanity, for even though prediction isn't my strong suit, it seems to me we've reached a critical turning point, and what happens in the next twenty years will determine the fate of our species.

Before your soul entered your body it was communing with spirit in a state of oneness. After you depart that body you'll return to spirit. You came from love and are carrying love back to love, though it doesn't always look that way. Like deep-sea fish, we swim through love our whole lives and don't know it, because how could a fish know water?

From having spent long hours peering into human beings, I've learned there's infinitely more to everyone than meets the eye. Even when you're lost and hopeless, some part of you isn't. Even when you're about to give up, your ruby heart may just be getting started.

Down at the hind end of the beast, when you get mashed by constricting coils of Dragontail that squeeze you inside stale energies and worn-out stories, you're not just wrestling with karma, you're sinking into parts of the soul where your willingness to find new stories can make all the difference between things going one way and another on this spinning blue-green jewel we ride through space.

Each of us has the whole zodiac inside. Each is following the footsteps of dragons who came before, and leaving footsteps for those who follow, on a path built by previous souls who wrestled the world monster to launch the flight of their own dragons.

If you feel stuck you can summon the sizzle of the first sign, Aries, to simplify your passage through the world like a finger pointing at the moon. You can dowse your way through the dense tangle of *Technotopia Moderna* in conjunction with life-giving forces. You can surf transformative currents that flush open channels for things to find each other in clear direct ways, shorn of unnecessary complications and excess thought. By dowsing energies that beam faster than thought, you can streamline your ride to the shortest distance between two points.

If deep peace and lasting meaning are currently lacking for you, like Taurus you can take time out, put your busy life on hold, until you find the sun, water and soil of creative purpose, clear flow of feelings and a life that feels good and works right. The three together would be sublime, but even if you only find two, you'll plant yourself in a rich garden of possibilities. The best way to grow in that garden is to open your heart to living life as an offering. When you live life as an offering, the accent switches from the things that haven't happened yet for you, to reaching back inside to deepen your offering. It's not your business to make sure how your offerings are received—it's just your business to keep offering them. In fact, the more poorly your devotion is accepted, the more purely you can dig down to raise it up again. When the world resists, clean the temple. When shadows lengthen, sweep the altar. Center your attention on what you have to give. Release the need to control what happens to your gifts after you give them. Stay close to the pristine spring running through the garden that keeps love alive.

As you go about gardening, if duality strikes and wholeness fractures, check to see if some dark double has convinced you that everything worth knowing is already known, and nothing significant is likely to change. Even stasis and depression become a mystic intersection when you invoke the sacred power of the crossroads to propel you like a dragon up and over the polarized view. When you fly out of duality, and then find a creative way to fly back in, the Gemini jetstream whips you around and around the lemniscate (the technical term for the infinity symbol) toward the satori of recognizing the oneness that contains duality. You harness that oneness when you inhabit the still clear point of diamond mind in the center where the two loops meet. Even though part of you keeps riding the rollercoaster, your deep mind becomes absolutely still, witnessing the craziness of life without getting hooked by any of it. Like Escher stairways, confounding perspectives that defied comprehension suddenly make sense, as you view them in a way that allows you to interact with duality from a nondual place. You get to be in the rollercoaster but no longer of it. You get to ride the rails with Rumi, who promised to meet us beyond the fields of polarization. And one day you may awaken to find duality, instead of being your worst enemy, has somehow become your best friend.

After returning from the flight of the dragon, where things were exalted by the dragon's lofty point of view, when you splatter back into the tidepools of everyday existence, if you find yourself dazed and confused, you can turn to *The Earth-User's Guide to Practical Human Being* and, like Cancer, read into the situation until learning what is and isn't yours. Once you fathom that, if something is still off, this may be your season of the soul to retire from the limelight and grow in the solitude underneath your shell before emerging out in the open. Exposing yourself now, much as you might want to, could be premature if you're not ready to deal with all the forces your emergence could stir up. You'd do better applying yourself to your next phase of internal growth. And the situation out there may not be ripe yet for what you have to give it, and could use another phase of its own.

Beneath this imperfect and perplexing life of yours a bush burns. Inside your belly a lion crouches. Before you had a body you were a soul, and that part of you is still intact. That part of you knows exactly who you are, where you've been, why you're here, where you're going and how to get there. Even though other parts of you forget, the lion in you never does, and is ready to steer by the light of that burning bush soon as you say the word. In your worst moments you're still a geyser of creativity who came here to yield revelations that throw back the darkness of the unlived life.

So many things in this world are not what they should be, but you can't allow yourself to be one of those things to the extent that you become contested territory. Between your depth nature and everyday self is a sovereign land that must be kept free of invasive energies and self-cancelling thought forms, where your inner truths can come to term. The more you inhabit that land, the better you'll hear the call of spirit when it comes, and the freer you'll be to dance with it. Your longing to dance with the light demands you dance with the darkness until learning what it and you are made of. Like Persephone in hell, once you claim your sacred ground, no external force can take it away. Transforming your dissatisfaction at what's not right into divine service is the great Virgo art. Right livelihood bestows the blessing of the virgin, which restores sacred rhythms in the midst of chaos, and clears channels of toxicity for love to stream through.

Many of us, similar to Libra, spend our lives searching for love. If you're on that ride, let your desperation to connect with another deepen the well of feeling within you. When there's no one out there to give your love to, aim it like a fire hose inside yourself to blow away the shadows of the past. Let your craving for a lover dissolve the barriers between your ego and your soul, allowing the immense love of creation to flow through. Let every one of love's blessings that hasn't yet happened for you turn your deeper passion on rather than sour you to the possibility of future happiness. If you've already found love, be willing to rediscover what it's made of. Existence is a great mirror that reflects whatever you bring to it. The more you recognize how much is always being given to you, the less you'll grasp and clutch to feed the hungry ghost.

The view from the scorpion's cave reveals that the colossal mess of our time was caused by damaged instincts. The giant scaly beast is waterlogged with wings folded on cold stone. We've become a world populated by human beings who no longer recognize deep and shallow truths. Repairing damaged instincts may be the most important job these days, because until you distinguish what you can't live without from what you can't stand, your dragon's at standstill. If the path outside your cave is blocked, go deeper in to find the love you're made of. Once you grant yourself the right to love what you love, need what you need and crave what you're obsessed with, your dragon will spread its wings and fly. If it ever gets trapped again just remember love isn't everything—it's the only thing.

Even when you're feeling small or alone, the Sagittarius in you knows life's an ecstatic celebration available to anyone willing to engage it that way. Like an Earth-sized archer, when you enter that festival, the physical plane pivots from being an obstacle course to a sumptuous feast. The dreams you dare to dream light the lanterns in the *Village of Many Names,* where kindred spirits gather to share food, music and conversation that make the world new again. Without growing another inch you're big as the Milky Way. Without earning another dollar, life's a banquet that magically increases its offerings the more you partake of them. When you feast upon the richness of the physical plane without getting jaded by it, and share the bounties of life without getting caged by them, your ride through fields of incarnation becomes a centaurian gallop, illuminated by the golden arrows that glow above the feast tables night after night.

Climbing the mountain of higher consciousness will raise your demons, scour your ego and pop your clever ideas apart. On that trek you'll lose the golden thread, get sidetracked, bust your shoes and stumble down the slopes more times than you can imagine, collapsing in a heap back where you started from. However, the eyes of the seagoat reveal those aren't wrong turns so much as proving grounds you needed to cross to learn their lessons and glean their gifts. The manifesting power of Capricorn enables you to plant one end of your consciousness in the sticky depths of your messy and incomprehensible existence, and anchor the other end way out in the far reaches of infinity. That karma-yogic stretch between the crunch of your dysfunction and apex of your vision strengthens you to recognize everything that happens as an invitation to awaken. Lost opportunities, frustrated signals and botched encounters yield self-mastery when love and understanding pour through.

Like Aquarius, your spirit is acclimated to wide-open fields. If your humanness, by comparison, feels cramped and puny, turn it into a vessel. It's not about you so much as what you tap and channel. The strongest brew in that bottle is love. When your soul came back from spirit it took a body the way an actor takes a role. Your willingness to play that role truthfully and magically is what fashions the vessel, and even imperfect vessels can channel a perfect force. The leap that the Water Bearer is summoning us to make is that all things are related to all other things, and all beings are related to all other beings. While every child knows this, it's not enough to know it, but to come alive inside that knowing to the extent that we sync up with universal intelligence and pass it on.

And when your vessel dissolves and your dragonflight ends, and you melt back into the Piscean sea, the universe will have irrevocably changed due to your passage through it. The channels you swim through on this side of the great divide mark the wake of your arrivals during a time of many departures and losses. Our species has forgotten what it's made of, and gotten marooned in strange disenchanted lives far from the waters of the soul. But the soul hasn't gone anywhere. Pisces is the ancient mariner in you standing strong, rising from the waves, casting a fishing line into the sea of incarnation to hook the great love everything's made of. If you can engage when others are disengaging, and love where love is hardest, the long-heralded, much-delayed arrival of your full presence in the depths of matter might just turn the tide for us all.

Most human lifetimes get strung together by karma, which provides continuity amidst the chaos and uncertainty that are now sweeping the world. Though it can weigh you down and restrict your movements, karmic necessity provides the rhythm track of your reincarnational dance with matter.

Without karma, your life would proceed like a rock song with keyboard, vocals and flute, but no bass and drums.

Your soul chose to land in a time, place and family it had karmic resonance with, among people who'd been covering similar ground in their own reincarnational journeys, with similar issues and challenges, which became the bass track of your current incarnation.

The places we fail to show up follow us around from life to life the way a dragon's tail follows its head, until we begin turning karma into grace by taking up the invitation to become present where we were absent, to become alert where we were checked out and to ignite where we were sputtering.

That invitation is hard to recognize and inner ignition is hard to achieve while we're caught in the tail of the dragon, captured by the shame, blame and judgment that keep the dark ages in place.

The greatest bondage of our age occurs when we turn against ourselves, on a fundamental, barely conscious level.

But even the densest karmas melt in the heat of the ruby heart of the dragon.

Old patterns of dysfunctional behavior that bound you in chains burst against the spreading of your scaly wings. Karmic wounds that throbbed along the reincarnational arc of your journey through the ages give way to streamlined flight.

Burdens that plagued you mark the scars where you got snagged by the convincing illusions of the physical plane. Such scars remind us that sometimes you first have to drop partway back into the illusion in order to get all the way out.

Maybe a thousand reruns of sexual dysfunction weren't enough, and you needed one more to wake up.

Maybe a thousand incidents of self-sabotage didn't burst your chains till you got chained one more time.

Because you forgot.

YOU FORGOT THAT YOU'RE GOD.

YOU FORGOT THAT YOU'RE *EVERYTHING* PRETENDING TO BE *SOMETHING*.

YOU FORGOT YOU HAVE THE WHOLE UNIVERSE INSIDE YOU.

YOU FORGOT THAT YOU'RE A DRAGON.

YOU LOST TOUCH WITH THE ELEMENTAL FORCES YOU'RE MADE OF.

It was a moment's flicker.

And after you and I have forgotten in enough different ways at enough different times and places in the Karmic Theater, perhaps we can spend the rest of our lives remembering.

And if we cross paths, flash a quick wink or knowing smile at me which acknowledges that everything is so much more than we'll ever realize, and the true story of what you're really made of could never fit into one small book or be contained in that little human body.

About the Author

MARK BORAX HAS BEEN A NOMADIC POET HIS WHOLE life. In the late Seventies he traveled the U.S. and Canada performing and selling his poetry. In the mid-Eighties, Mark was befriended by his adolescent idol Ray Bradbury, who became his literary godfather, believing in Mark's writing even though it was taking forever.

In 1984 he became a comic book writer and the managing editor of *Comics Interview* magazine. In 1987 he created Soul Level Astrology, which identifies the core nature and life purpose of individuals. In 1998 Mark rode his Harley Davidson through the U.S. and Europe, stopping for a year in the Tuscan countryside.

Mark's first book *2012: Crossing the Bridge to the Future* (soon to be republished as *Love, Sex & Astrology*) is a worldwide bestseller that describes the author's seven-year apprenticeship to visionary astrologer Ellias Lonsdale. Under the Redwoods of northern California, they created a mystery school where Lonsdale birthed a new form of astrology called Star Genesis.

Mark's second book (co-authored with Lonsdale) is a *Cosmic Weather Report* that inspires readers to rethink the whole purpose of humankind.

In 2008, Mark and his wife Marcella Eversole founded The College of Visionaries & Wizards, which teaches students around the world to live by the soul, and to read charts the magical way Mark does.

Mark is also a singer-songwriter who combines his live music with lecture in a method he calls starjazz.

To learn more about Mark and his work, to book a soul session or sign up for his free monthly Cosmic Weather Report, visit markborax.com.

For information on The College of Visionaries & Wizards, where Mark and Marcella teach live online classes, visit soullevelastrology.com.

To purchase the companion series of podcasts that illuminate sections of this book as a reader's guide, visit therubyheartofthedragon.com, where you can also find out about the ebook and audio editions.

Mark Borax and Blackie, his 1998 Low Rider, on his Harley ride.
(Photo by Luca Carena)

Acknowledgments

THANKS TO ALEJANDRA SOPHIA, FOR SPARKING THE INItial version of this book, and Kathy Glass, my impeccable editor, for polishing it. Thanks to A.J. Harper for encouraging and coaching me to self-publish. Big shout out to Amber Vilhauer and NGNG, who upped my game and spread word of my work. Thanks to Robin McManus who years ago told me she couldn't wait for this book. Many thanks to Peter Selgin for the cover art, and to Olaf Nelson for the dragony and outstanding page design and logo. Deep gratitude to Ann DeSutter for checking my date numbers in the back. Thanks to all our current students and graduates in The College of Visionaries & Wizards for letting me captain your voyage through the soul side of the stars. Thanks to CVW Angels Brooke Kelly, Kathy Grace and Sheridan Kennedy for strongly supporting my work and our school. Thanks to Keidren Devas, Duncan Mackenzie, Pam Forman, Kayhan Irani, Mireya Alejo, Alessandra Bosco, Lynne Patrice, Steffon Moody, Mary Webb and Deborah Koff Chapin for listening in on my early chapter development. Heartfelt thanks to Shay Marie who helped me learn how to at long last treat Virgo the way she deserves. Most of all—deep thanks to my ecstatic wife Marcella, for indefatigably championing my work and for never failing to believe in the great goodness of all things, and to my children Rowan Hart and Sky, for shining your ruby hearts on mine in this wild ride through incarnation during the craziest time on planet Earth.

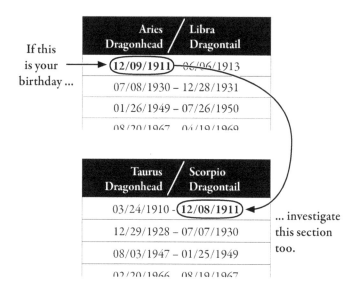

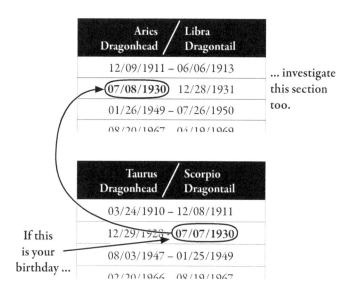

Appendix: How to Identify Your Dragonhead and Tail

NOTE THAT THE FOLLOWING INFORMATION DOESN'T PERtain to your Sun sign but your north and south nodes.

This information is based on birthdays but not birth places or hours, so in some cases it may not be accurate. If your birthday falls between the listed birthdays you can count on the information being accurate.

But if your exact birthdate appears in the tables below (rather than falling between the printed dates) you should check with an astrologer to see whether you really belong there or in an adjacent section. Alternatively, instead of checking with an astrologer, you can read the description of the adjacent section in the chapter endpage pertaining to those two adjacent signs, and see if it feels like a better fit.

There are two such scenarios, illustrated on the previous page.

If your birthday is the first date in a line (let's use the first Aries/Libra date, 12/09/1911, as an example) you may wish to drop down to the next section where you'll find the previous day (12/08/1911, in Taurus/Scorpio). Read the Taurus/Scorpio information *and* the Aries/Libra information and try them both on for size.

If your birthday is the second date in its line (like 07/07/1930 in the second line of Taurus/Scorpio) you can rise up and find the subsequent date in the section above it (07/08/1930, in the second line of Aries/Libra), do some reading and see what suits you better.

Aries Dragonhead / Libra Dragontail
12/09/1911 – 06/06/1913
07/08/1930 – 12/28/1931
01/26/1949 – 07/26/1950
08/20/1967 – 04/19/1969
04/07/1986 – 12/02/1987
12/26/2004 – 06/21/2006
07/18/2023 – 01/11/2025
02/04/2042 – 08/18/2043

Cancer Dragonhead / Capricorn Dragontail
03/31/1907 – 09/27/1908
10/27/1925 – 04/16/1927
05/12/1944 – 12/02/1945
12/24/1962 – 08/25/1964
09/21/1981 – 09/21/1981
09/25/1981 – 03/16/1983
04/09/2000 – 10/12/2001
11/07/2018 – 05/04/2020
05/29/2037 – 02/09/2039

Taurus Dragonhead / Scorpio Dragontail
03/24/1910 – 12/08/1911
12/29/1928 – 07/07/1930
08/03/1947 – 01/25/1949
02/20/1966 – 08/19/1967
09/12/1984 – 04/06/1986
04/14/2003 – 12/25/2004
01/19/2022 – 07/17/2023
08/11/2040 – 02/03/2042

Leo Dragonhead / Aquarius Dragontail
09/19/1905 – 03/30/1907
04/23/1924 – 10/26/1925
11/22/1942 – 05/11/1944
06/11/1961 – 12/23/1962
01/06/1980 – 01/07/1980
01/13/1980 – 09/20/1981
09/22/1981 – 09/24/1981
10/21/1998 – 04/08/2000
05/10/2017 – 11/06/2018
11/30/2035 – 05/28/2037

Gemini Dragonhead / Sagittarius Dragontail
09/28/1908 – 03/23/1910
04/17/1927 – 12/28/1928
12/03/1945 – 08/02/1947
08/26/1964 – 02/19/1966
03/17/1983 – 09/11/1984
10/13/2001 – 04/13/2003
05/05/2020 – 01/18/2022
02/10/2039 – 08/10/2040

Virgo Dragonhead / Pisces Dragontail
01/16/1904 – 09/18/1905
08/23/1922 – 08/27/1922
09/01/1922 – 04/22/1924
05/25/1941 – 11/21/1942
12/16/1959 – 06/10/1961
07/06/1978 – 01/05/1980
01/08/1980 – 01/12/1980
01/26/1997 – 10/20/1998
11/12/2015 – 05/09/2017
06/04/2034 – 11/29/2035

Libra Dragonhead / Aries Dragontail
07/22/1902 – 01/15/1904
02/08/1921 – 08/22/1922
08/28/1922 – 08/31/1922
09/12/1939 – 05/24/1941
06/17/1958 – 12/15/1959
01/08/1977 – 07/05/1978
08/01/1995 – 01/25/1997
02/19/2014 – 11/11/2015
12/02/2032 – 06/03/2034

Capricorn Dragonhead / Cancer Dragontail
06/01/1916 – 02/13/1918
03/09/1935 – 09/14/1936
10/10/1953 – 04/02/1955
04/28/1972 – 10/27/1973
11/19/1990 – 08/01/1992
08/22/2009 – 03/03/2011
03/27/2028 – 09/23/2029
10/19/2046 – 04/11/2048

Scorpio Dragonhead / Taurus Dragontail
01/21/1901 – 07/21/1902
08/16/1919 – 02/07/1921
03/04/1938 – 09/11/1939
10/05/1956 – 06/16/1958
07/11/1975 – 01/07/1977
02/02/1994 – 07/31/1995
08/30/2012 – 02/18/2014
03/21/2031 – 12/01/2032
12/14/2049 – 12/20/2049

Aquarius Dragonhead / Leo Dragontail
12/04/1914 – 05/31/1916
06/25/1933 – 03/08/1935
03/29/1952 – 10/09/1953
11/03/1970 – 04/27/1972
05/23/1989 – 11/18/1990
12/15/2007 – 12/15/2007
12/18/2007 – 08/21/2009
07/27/2026 – 03/26/2028
04/19/2045 – 10/18/2046

Sagittarius Dragonhead / Gemini Dragontail
05/10/1899 – 01/20/1901
02/14/1918 – 08/15/1919
09/15/1936 – 03/03/1938
04/03/1955 – 10/04/1956
10/28/1973 – 07/10/1975
08/02/1992 – 02/01/1994
03/04/2011 – 08/29/2012
09/24/2029 – 03/20/2031
04/12/2048 – 12/13/2049
12/21/2049 – 12/22/2049

Pisces Dragonhead / Virgo Dragontail
06/07/1913 – 12/03/1914
12/29/1931 – 06/24/1933
07/27/1950 – 03/28/1952
04/20/1969 – 11/02/1970
12/03/1987 – 05/22/1989
06/22/2006 – 12/14/2007
12/16/2007 – 12/17/2007
01/12/2025 – 07/26/2026
08/19/2043 – 04/18/2045

Ingram Content Group UK Ltd.
Milton Keynes UK
UKHW040639090723
424792UK00004B/58

9 798987 771105